COMING HOME WHOLE

COMING HOME WHOLE

A Draftee's Foretold Journey To and From Vietnam

Don Graham

Valley of the Moon Press

Valley of the Moon Press
valleyofthemoonpress@gmail.com

Coming Home Whole:
A Draftee's Foretold Journey to and from Vietnam

© 2018 by Donald S. Graham

All rights reserved. This book or any portion thereof may not be reproduced or used in any manner whatsoever without the express written permission of the author except for the use of brief quotations in a book review. For permission requests, contact valleyofthemoonpress@gmail.com.

ISBN 978-0-692-06741-3
Book design by cj Madigan, Shoebox Stories
Cover art and crossroads image by Matt Graham

*This book is dedicated to
two remarkable women
who have shaped this story and my life:
my mother, Ruth,
and my wife, MaryAnne*

In 1968, America was a wounded nation. The wounds were moral ones; the Vietnam War and three summers of inner-city riots had inflicted them on the national soul, challenging Americans' belief that they were a uniquely noble and honorable people.
    —Thurston Clark

In all chaos there is a cosmos, in all disorder a secret order.
    —Carl Jung

Coincidence is God's way of remaining anonymous.
    —Albert Einstein

There is no Satan or hell. The potential for evil resides in each of us. When I am fighting the battle within myself, feelings of fear and anger are often directed at others. It is helpful if I keep in mind that most everyone is doing the best they know how, including me.
    —Don Graham

I'm gonna lay down my sword and shield
Down by the riverside
I'm gonna study war no more
    —Traditional Spiritual

CONTENTS

PROLOGUE: WARS AND PEACE 1
1 COULD THIS BE A SIGN? 3
2 All IN THE FAMILY 11
3 THE WOMEN IN MY LIFE 21
4 IT'S ALL IN THE WRIST 29
5 DALY CITY—VISIBILITY ZERO 38
6 LIFE AT THE MINI-RANCH 44
7 OH CANADA 52
8 DRAFTED ON ELECTION DAY 61
9 GETTING DOWN TO BASICS 66
10 WHAT A BLAST! 78
11 WHEN I SAY JUMP... 86
12 WELCOME TO THE WAR 96
13 GUNS BUT NO ROSES 110

14 WHO KNOWS WHAT'S IN THE CARDS?   122

15 STAYING SANE IN A CRAZY PLACE   129

16 CAN I CATCH A BREAK?   138

17 FROM THE HILL OF THE ANGELS   145

18 NEXT STOP, PARADISE   151

19 WHAT'S UP, DOC?   157

20 TWENTY QUESTIONS   164

21 WELCOME THE NEW ARRIVAL   173

22 AIN'T GONNA STUDY WAR NO MORE   183

EPILOGUE: RETURNS AND REFLECTIONS   190

APPENDIX: ABOUT THE 110 HEAVY HOWITZER   197

AUTHOR'S NOTE AND ACKNOWLEGEMENTS   201

ABOUT THE AUTHOR   203

END NOTES   205

PROLOGUE

The time was the late 1960s, a period of tremendous upheaval in the United States. The nation was heavily involved in what were essentially three civil wars—one a civil war in a literal sense and the others civil wars in metaphorical terms.

The civil war between North and South Vietnam had been going on since the 1950s. America's increasingly deep and costly involvement in that conflict led to another civil war of sorts on our own shores. Those who supported the war and the government that pursued it clashed verbally and sometimes physically with those who were anti-war, anti-government or both. Families and communities were divided, with splits that sometimes took a generation or more to heal. Indeed, despite all the analysis and the soul-searching that has gone on in the intervening years, many Americans still disagree on the necessity, justice, and cost of the Vietnam War.

The third of these civil wars, metaphorically speaking, was the surging conflict over civil rights that exploded in the 1960s. That had been going on since the 19th century, and events including the Rodney King riots and the emergence of the Black Lives Matter movement suggest that it continues to this day.

These three roiling conflicts were the intense cultural and emotional backdrop against which I came of age. I didn't consciously choose to be part of any of them, yet I was touched by all three to a greater or lesser extent.

Along the way, they engaged me in a fourth civil war: an inner battle, a war between my own conflicting expectations and beliefs.

This is the story of that inner battle…of the life and times that gave rise to it…and of the forces, often mysterious or unseen, which kept me whole and helped me find my way to peace.

1

COULD THIS BE A SIGN?

It was a beautiful day in the summer of 1968, and I was full of anticipation. I had been accepted to a master's program in psychology at California State University at Chico, further education that genuinely appealed to me even beyond its role in helping me avoid the draft. My wife of one year, MaryAnne, and I would be renting a very small house at something-and-a-half Cherry Street, not far from the campus. An agricultural town 90 miles north of Sacramento, Chico was best known for the university that sits in its center. The Chico State campus is one of the oldest in California, built around a 19th-century estate and full of ivy-covered brick buildings and graceful trees. Now, a week after we had signed our lease, I was driving the first load of our belongings from Napa to Chico while MaryAnne continued to pack up and organize the old place.

I was driving north on Highway 99 in my in-laws' Dodge Lancer station wagon, cruising at around 65 mph or so through the farmland of the Sacramento Valley. As I got closer to the larger station wagon ahead of me a few miles south of Chico, I turned my attention from the songs on the radio to the car and its invisible driver. He drifted somewhat to the right and went a bit off the road but then came back on. I watched him carefully for a minute or two, and he seemed to have recovered from whatever had bothered him and was driving just fine. Still, I didn't know if the driver ahead of me was drunk or sleepy or what. Whatever it was, it made me a little nervous. So I decided that I would rather be in front of him than behind him.

In those days, Highway 99 was only one lane in each direction. I waited for an opportunity to pass, and when I saw it was clear, I pulled out into the other lane and stepped on the gas. As my front bumper drew even with its rear bumper, the station wagon once again went off the road into the gravel, then spun around back into the middle of the road in front of me. I swerved to the left in an attempt to avoid a collision, but the rear of his vehicle hit the rear of the Lancer and sent me spinning in the opposite direction. The Lancer spun across the road and hit a power pole on the passenger's side at what must have been about 50 mph. Spinning some more, it finally came to a stop on the side of the road. When the dust settled, I found myself facing back in the direction from which I had come.

The other vehicle in this now completed mechanical ballet was on its side in the middle of the highway. A boy was just beginning to climb up and out through an open window. The accident had happened so fast that I hardly had time to react. All I could do was hang on for dear life. It was a wild ride, and scary as hell. I was probably in shock, but as I sat there, the reality of the situation began to dawn on me.

The radio was on, which meant the ignition was on, which meant there was a possibility of a spark that could ignite any leaking gasoline. I didn't know if the gas was leaking, but after a crash of this magnitude I wouldn't be surprised. I knew I had to get out of the car, and quickly! I turned off the ignition. Since the driver's door wouldn't open, I jumped into the back and tried one of the doors there. Again, no luck. So I started kicking on the back door to get it open. I was able to open it enough to jump out. Some other drivers had now stopped to help. I wanted to get away from my car, but instead a Good Samaritan decided that I should sit down and rest, up against the front tire of my car. Or, rather, my in-law's car —a car that I had just destroyed. But, despite his best intentions, I just knew I wanted to get some distance from that car, so I got up and walked away.

As I surveyed our belongings strewn from hell to breakfast across the highway, I found it all a bit surreal. Getting into automobile accidents was new to me. I was (and am) not accustomed to having to consider whether or not a car might be about to blow up in my immediate vicinity; I have no experience with seeing all of my worldly possessions littering a public highway. And yet, here I was, and there was the smashed car, and there were my wife's clothing, my modest collection of books, our sewing machine and more—all now decorating Highway 99.

Needless to say, I was still in a daze and certainly in no shape to be picking up these items. Besides, I didn't have a car to put them in.

Then another Samaritan approached me and offered me a ride to the local emergency room. With encouragement from others who had stopped, I accepted the offer. I knew I was not seriously hurt in any physical way, but I agreed with the notion that I was in shock. On the way to the hospital the reality of having just totaled my in-laws' automobile began to sink in big time. A combination of guilt and anxiety began to flood over me. I began to worry about how they would react when they got the news. This was foolish of me. My in-laws are kind and loving people, and I concluded they would be more concerned about me than the car.

I also wondered how the people in the other vehicle had fared. It seemed like there were a lot of them in the car. I had no idea if any of them were hurt. I wanted to see the driver of the other car, for I was puzzled and curious as to why they had gone off the road, but it was too late for that.

The emergency room was unremarkable. Certainly, it was modern enough, with all the standard emergency-room furnishings and apparatus, all of which had clearly been well used but were not overly worn. As one would reasonably expect, it came with that familiar hospital smell of disinfectant mixed with other medicinal odors.

The ER doctor checked me over and found little wrong with me. I had a small cut above my eyebrow that took a stitch or two and an abrasion on my left knee where my leg had hit the emergency-brake handle. The doctor also said that my right eardrum was ruptured.

I called MaryAnne in Napa from a pay phone. "MaryAnne, I have some really bad news. I've been in an accident and the Lancer is totaled."

"What?!"

"I'm in the emergency room at Community Hospital in

Chico. They've checked me out and I'm fine—just a couple of scratches."

"Really? You're okay?"

"Really! I'm fine. But the car's totaled."

"What happened?"

"Someone sort of ran me off the road. I'll explain the whole thing when I see you. But I need you to drive up to Chico and pick me up."

Naturally, she was upset and concerned, but she agreed to drive to Chico and get me.

I wanted to go check on my belongings and see what happened to them. I had no way to do that and felt rather helpless until I thought to call my new landlord. It really lifted my spirits when he said he would be right down. While I was waiting, a highway patrolman came in looking for me. He looked to be in his early 50s, balding with glasses and carrying the ever-present notepad. I was a bit fearful when I first saw him. I didn't know what anyone had told him about the accident—how it occurred or who was at fault. I felt a whole lot better when the officer told me that no one in the other car was hurt and that he was clear that it wasn't my fault. However, he had to ask some questions in order to complete his report. As it turned out, all his questions were strictly routine, and I felt a good deal better when we were through.

My landlord showed up shortly afterward and drove me to the auto dealer in Chico, where they had towed my car. As we entered the shop, we were approached by a young employee who asked how he could help us. I told him that I had come to retrieve my belongings, that my car was the white Lancer station wagon. He looked at me with wide eyes and said,

"You were in that car? I didn't expect to see anyone from it walking in here!"

When I saw the remains of the Lancer, I was pretty amazed. The entire passenger side of the car had been bashed in by the power pole. The windshield and side windows were shattered, and the tailgate was clearly inoperable. I felt lucky and very thankful. I was delighted to see that someone had gathered up all my strewn belongings and had put them in the back seat. I was also greatly saddened by the condition of our belongings after they had been scattered across the highway at high speed.

The reality of what this might mean to my in-laws began to sink in. MaryAnne's folks still had five children at home between the ages of eight and seventeen. One less vehicle would definitely complicate their lives for a while. I couldn't help but feel guilty, even though I knew the accident wasn't my fault.

When MaryAnne, accompanied by her brother Bill, showed up in a VW "Bug" to give me a ride home, it was clear that she was very shaken. She ran up and threw her arms around me.

"What the heck happened? Are you sure you're all right? Tell me the truth." So I explained what had happened and assured her that I was just fine. However, a sizable part of me couldn't help but think of how I might easily have died that afternoon. Clearly, it was just not my time.

After a two-and-a-half-hour drive back home from Chico to Napa through the varied agriculture of the Sacramento Valley floor, Bill turned the VW onto the long, dusty driveway that led to the house where MaryAnne and I lived. A small cottage on the southern outskirts of Napa, it had come to be known in our families as the "mini-ranch." The ride home had been uneventful until we stopped at the mailboxes. Still in the car, Bill retrieved and handed me a handful of mail. Once inside the house I began to sort through it.

As I sorted, I came across an envelope that was all too official looking from the federal government. As soon as I saw it, I knew what it was. As I opened it, I saw that it was just as I feared. I was filled with a combination of dread and disbelief. I had known it would come one of these days, but today? After all I had been through today? Unbelievable! MaryAnne saw the look on my face, and I handed her the draft notice.

I was speechless, filled with so many emotions that I couldn't sort them all out. After the initial surprise, I felt mostly anger, then despair. My mind reeled as I asked myself, "Is someone trying to send me a message regarding my plans for grad school?" MaryAnne was in tears. I knew this would be a difficult night. We were in shock. Up until now our life together had been charmed. We assumed that awful things were not supposed to happen to us. This was a harsh dose of reality.

Disappointment and fear make for a regrettable combination. The expectation of moving to something-and-a-half Cherry Street in Chico was now replaced with the prospect of being separated by war. We would never live on Cherry Street, as it turned out. There was little to say. It was a quiet and tearful night.

The next day I went down to the draft board to see Alice. Neither the exterior nor the interior of this building gave any clue as to the heart-wrenching judgments that were passed down here. It had the appearance of a standard business office. Alice and I were on a first-name basis, since I'd been avoiding the draft for five years with student deferments. She was an attractive woman of around 40 with long brown hair and a pleasant smile. I entered with a growing sense of doom, anticipating the worst. The grinding gears of the bureaucracy would not disappoint. I said, "Alice, what's the story?" She said, "Don, you're the oldest eligible person on our lists. If the quota for Napa County next month is one person, you're it."

My mind reviewed the game of cat and mouse that we had played for the past five years. I ticked off the various alternative escape routes that I had considered over time. I'd exhausted educational deferments. The other options—maiming myself, considering conscientious objector status or emigration, persuading a psychiatrist that I was emotionally unstable—were all fruitless, though I'd only recently closed the door on a final alternative, going to prison for refusing the draft. There were no degrees of freedom left. The only option I could see was to submit.

I hung my head, slowly raised my hands in the air and told Alice, "I give up."

2

ALL IN THE FAMILY

Like so many young men of my time, I was an unlikely candidate for draft dodging. The mother who raised me was many things: a survivor, someone fascinated by spirituality, an artist, and also a patriot who worked for many years on a naval base. She had been orphaned at the age of 12 when her own mother died in a fire. Since no relative chose to take her in, she became a ward of the court and ended up working her way through high school as hired help in well-to-do homes. She was very bright, an avid reader who was fascinated by various religious philosophies and who had a natural gift for teaching. She hoped to attend college after graduating from high school, but higher education was still seen as a privilege rather than a norm, much less a right. The consensus was that as someone without family support of any kind, she needed to do something more practical.

In response, she attended secretarial school and, at the age of 19, went to work as a messenger at Mare Island Naval Shipyard in Vallejo, California. Just a few miles south of Napa and a little more than 20 miles from San Francisco,

Mare Island is actually a peninsula despite its name, being separated from the mainland only by seasonal water flows. After being reserved for military use in 1850 by President Millard Fillmore, Mare Island had become a naval shipyard and, in 1854, the first permanent U.S. military base on the West Coast.

My mother, Ruth, met my father in Vallejo in 1944. "Five foot-two, eyes of blue," she was working in a clerical position at Mare Island by then. My father, Edward Russell Graham, known as Red, was a skinny red-haired aspiring musician about five feet six inches tall. He'd been sent from Massachusetts to Vallejo along with the rest of his army division, the 211th, to guard the naval base there. But he did very little real guarding, as his unit was actually a military band in which he played saxophone and clarinet. Music was Red's first and perhaps only love, a passion that I'm sure he wished that he could pursue as a profession rather than just as a hobby.

Mom and Red met and things clicked for them. They married in 1944. His division was sent to Fort Hood, Texas, where I was born in 1945. The war ended shortly thereafter, and the troops mostly went home. Home for my father was Ashland, Massachusetts, where we arrived with the first snow of the season. At this point my father apparently said, "I've seen California and I can't take any more Massachusetts winters. I'm going back to California." He moved our small family back to Vallejo when I was one. He took at job at the Bank of America, as his passion for music didn't earn him a living,

The marriage got rocky over time, and my mother filed for divorce when I was three years old. One of my earliest

Mom and I, 1949

memories is standing in my parents' bedroom watching my father throwing things into a suitcase. I stood there confused and upset. That's when I became the man of the house.

Looking back, I think that my father was basically a good man and, by all reports, a good friend. But he was also someone not cut out to be a father or a husband. He gave up the father routine at the time he left our house. And he bailed on the husband routine a few years later, at the time of his second divorce. He came to see me maybe three times a year, although he only lived about 18 miles away and I was his only child.

My chief memory of him during childhood is disappointment. Between the ages of six and eight I remember numerous days on which I would sit on the curb, clean and neatly dressed, waiting for my father to appear. I waited, and I waited, but he was often a no-show. Eventually my mother would come out of the house and explain to me he would not be coming today. I learned not to expect very much, but that's a hard lesson for any kid. I don't remember feeling angry but rather, disappointed and hurt.

I seldom saw my father in the years that followed. Looking back, I believe his absence had a significant effect on me, but of course I wasn't conscious of that at the time. Its immediate effect was to help turn me into what was generally labeled a "behavior problem" and bring my mother to numerous parent-teacher conferences. I was interested in making the other kids laugh rather than causing pain, but my antics were disruptive anyway.

My partner in crime was a boy named Dick Hathaway, who felt like a brother before I had actual brothers of my own. My mother and his had been best friends since they had met as messengers on the naval base. He and I spent so much time together that we were practically brothers. When my mother remarried when I was five, we moved to my stepfather's home in Napa, and I didn't see Dick for three years. Then his family moved in next door to us in Napa, and once again we were like brothers.

My mother was a spiritual questioner and seeker, someone whose lifelong interest in the unseen spanned a wide spectrum of faiths and practices. My new stepfather, Leigh Hein, wasn't particularly religious, and my mother determined that the only church he would be likely to attend would be Catholic. Knowing this, she joined the Catholic Church when I was nine. In the years before Vatican II the Church was more inflexible and forbidding than it has become, expecting obedience to its rules and bestowing punishments, including excommunication, on those who rebelled. But though my mother was willing to convert, it was her style to adapt Catholicism to her own worldview rather than succumbing to the kind of blind faith that may have been expected.

As the education required for converts progressed, she peppered local priests with questions about Church doctrine and spiritual matters. When they couldn't answer, she was sent for an audience with the bishop in San Francisco. She was clearly something of a puzzle to him. Later, I learned that he told her, "You are either an instrument of the devil or a very gifted spiritual woman." Despite this, she was duly accepted as a Catholic. Under the Church's Pauline privilege, which made limited allowances for the dissolutions of previous marriages between unbaptized individuals, my mother and Leigh were married in the Church despite her earlier marriage and divorce.

My new stepfather had serious health problems. Despite undergoing 20 or so major operations, the bone disease from which he suffered caused him constant pain. Though he was a good man and a good provider, his good moods were few and far between. A cab driver when he met my mother, he realized that he needed a better job to support the family. He faked his way into a job as a machinist, a field in which he had great natural gifts but no actual training. He taught himself while on the job. For years I watched him work eight hours on one job, come home to eat dinner, and then go work a four-hour shift at another job just to make ends meet. It was a grueling schedule for a man in constant pain.

My mother too made sacrifices to make sure that our family was stable. In between breaks for child rearing she continued to work clerical jobs at Mare Island, making that base—and the military generally—one of the constants of her life. During the Second World War years, Mare Island had employed 18,500 workers—including 400 naval architects, engineers and draftsmen—and held shipbuilding and repair facilities as well as a naval hospital with almost 600 beds. During the Vietnam years it remained a significant military location. The shallow, shifting nature of Mare Island's surrounding waters made it an ideal training site for the kinds of "brown water" navigation and crafts needed for combat in Vietnam. The navy moved its riverine training operations there in the 1960s.

I was nine and an only child when my brother Mark was born. My mother and stepfather had apparently hoped for a girl; so, they tried again and along came Paul. At that point, they gave up trying. After being an only child for so long, I had mixed feelings about siblings. There was a definite shift of attention toward the young kids. Yet I enjoyed them and had fun teaching them.

My brothers were both extremely bright, though in ways that were quite distinct when we were young. Mark could read before he turned five and was clearly ahead of most children his age. He was extremely verbal and self-assured. On the other hand, Paul struggled with a learning disorder that wasn't discovered until he was in the fourth grade and took some years to overcome. I remember him as shy and quiet but a sweet child who loved to laugh. Both Mark and Paul went on to become successful and highly capable men.

As for me, I was generally self-confident and knew that I was bright compared to most kids in my classes, although I frequently got by without much effort and was classified as an underachiever.

If ours wasn't a particularly happy home due to my stepfather's chronic pain, it wasn't unhappy, either. My mother did the best she could to cheer things up. Naturally playful, she loved to laugh and had a great sense of fun. She loved the rituals and generosity of Christmas and also relished Halloween. Having been born on October 31, she laughingly claimed to be a good—"white"—witch. She was also very artistic, painting in oils late at night once the family was in bed.

When I was 15, my stepfather underwent his 21st major operation. Fearing that he wouldn't live through it, he gave his sons wheels. He bought me a used car, Mark a new bike and Paul a new trike. To his surprise, he lived through the surgery only to be faced with a 15-year-old son with a car. Oops! I was caught by the police for having pushed my car down the street late at night to go joyriding. It wasn't the only time I did that, just the only time I got caught. It was a great temptation for a 15-year-old male.

My stepfather's health improved markedly after that operation, and so did the general tenor of the household. He felt well enough then to be a Scout leader. I was a member of the Boy Scouts and then the Explorer Scouts. My teenage years were basically happy. I enjoyed middle school and high school, especially athletics and social events. Like many boys I was mainly interested in sports, cars and girls, not necessarily in that order. I loved rock 'n roll music and enjoyed dancing. My folks and I got along reasonably well. I never went through a rebellious stage. I was becoming more interested in spirituality but wasn't conventionally religious; my biggest connection to the Church was as a member of the Catholic youth organization. I even spent a year as president of the club. Although I loved my little brothers, I didn't spend a lot of time with them. I was busy being a teenager and at the time, the decade between us proved to be quite a gap.

Though the official beginning of the Vietnam conflict dates to 1950, neither the central role it would play in American life nor the resistance it later engendered was on the average American's radar for some years thereafter. The Korean War was not popular, but few refused to serve; the so-called Cold War and the might of the Soviet Union felt like a real and present danger.

As someone who had come through World War II—a war

that had America fully behind it—and who now worked on a bustling military base, my mother regarded the military in a positive light. As far back as I can remember she repeatedly told me that I was fortunate to be born in the United States, and if my country ever called me, it was my duty to serve. Over the years I took this lesson to heart. While in high school I thought I might join the Reserve Officers' Training Corps, or ROTC, when I got to college. It seemed like a reasonable idea to graduate from college and be qualified to be an officer in the military—I could envision myself in a Marine Corps officer's uniform. During the 1963 Cuban Missile Crisis, which occurred during the latter half of my senior year of high school, my friends and I felt fully prepared to cross the street to the military recruitment office. Luckily, the Russians didn't break through America's naval embargo, but had they done so I was ready and eager to fight.

At about the same time, as I approached high school graduation, my parents got a surprise. My mother was pregnant with Mary, my only sister. Aged 40, Mom might have died in childbirth delivering Mary if it weren't for the fact that she just happened to be at the doctor's office getting a checkup when she began to hemorrhage. Timing is everything. Mom really enjoyed having a girl at last. Being about 19 years older than Mary, my relationship to her was almost that of an uncle. By the time she was beginning to talk I was moving out of the house to attend college. Despite that, there was never any doubt that she and I had a strong connection.

From early on Mary loved sports and all types of games. And she would gradually begin to share my mother's great interest in all things spiritual.

My biological father finally developed an interest in me when I was a teenager, maybe because by then I could hold an adult conversation. Unfortunately, by that time I had begun to lose interest in him. Leigh played the role of a father figure well, I was occupied with my own life, and I had been disappointed too often to feel connected to Red. At that point he was gone on the road for the bank 10 months out of the year, so I didn't see him much anyway.

3

THE WOMEN IN MY LIFE

I wasn't fully aware of it as a child or even teenager, but my mother grappled with a lot of inner pain during my younger years. The strict religion in which she was raised, the lack of a stable family or home in childhood, and her divorce from my father—an act that, at the time, she saw as damning her to Hell—all took their toll. Years later she explained to me that she believed that either her mind or her body was going to break in some way because of the stress.

As a single mother trying to raise and support a child on her own, she had developed a case of hives. The hives, and the terrible itching that went along with them, spread all over her body. Available treatments didn't seem to help, and as our sole support, she had to keep working full time. She had to live with the condition with little relief. She had not been sleeping and was at her wit's end when, on a Friday afternoon, a friend at work said, "I bet David could help you."

Mom said, "I've been to a couple of doctors. At this point I would see a witch doctor if I thought he could help."

After work that day she left me with a friend and headed

for Los Angeles. David Bruton (not to be confused with the British psychic and spiritualist of the same name) was waiting on the lawn when they arrived. He was a metaphysician but worked as a chiropractor. He said he used chiropractic adjustments to convince people that he had "done something" physical to create a change, which opened their minds to the possibility of healing. He gave my mother an adjustment and told her to go lie down and sleep. She said, "I haven't been able to sleep in days." When she lay down, she went right to sleep and slept for hours. When she awoke, the rash was already going away.

At the time of my mother's healing I was only three years old. I had been diagnosed with a diverticulum—an inflamed pocket in the intestine—that I am told is very unusual for a child that age. I won't go into the specifics and the symptoms. The medical doctors had told my mother that I was too young for corrective surgery. That would have to wait. Meanwhile, the condition caused me considerable pain and distress. When my mother described the condition to David, he asked her to bring me to see him in Los Angeles. I only vaguely recall his office but I do remember the ceramic frog he kept on his desk. He put me on his chiropractic table and gave me one treatment, commenting that I was very receptive to the healing. I've had no similar problems in all the decades since. I have no way of knowing for sure, but I believe I had a serious physiological malady that David permanently corrected.

There is an old saying: "When the student is ready, the teacher will appear." For my mother, this was the beginning of a long-distance spiritual teacher-student relationship that lasted seven years, until David passed on. I still have the copy of his book that my mother owned.[1]

I was a child during that time, but when I was older, she recounted a number of spiritual experiences that I'm sure most people would consider unusual. We certainly did, but we both trusted them anyway.

One unusual event she described was when she went into her bedroom to get a shawl. As she stood facing the mirror, she saw a figure pass behind her and heard the words, "Grandma was here tonight." At the same time she also saw a beautiful rose.

An experience she had with David took place at a social gathering where my mother and David were at opposite ends of the room. My mother was engaged in conversation when suddenly she heard a very loud sound, as though someone had clapped his or her hands vigorously right next to her ear. As she looked around to see what had caused the noise, she saw David at the other end of the room smiling at her. No one had clapped his or her hands. David was merely making a point.

In another instance, there was a time when she had ongoing back pain and wrote a letter to David asking if he could help. She was at work one afternoon when, all of a sudden, her back pain ceased. She was very surprised and looked at the clock, thinking that it was perhaps just temporary relief. It was roughly 3 o'clock. As the day went on, the relief continued. A few days later she received a letter from David apologizing for the delay and noting that he had not opened his mail that day until 3 o'clock.

One day while she and I were discussing the issue of reincarnation, my mother revealed something to me she had never shared previously. She explained that while she and my father were courting, she became pregnant and my father insisted that she have an abortion. This was before *Roe v. Wade* and back-alley abortions were common. They were living in Vallejo at the time. She sought out a doctor in San Francisco to have this done. While she was on the table during the procedure her heart stopped beating. She explained that she found herself essentially floating near the ceiling, looking down at her body, and the nurse who was frantically trying to revive her. Shortly thereafter she reentered her body. The nurse was most relieved that my mother's heart was beating again. I was naturally startled to hear this story, but she wasn't finished. She explained that my brother Mark had come to her one day when he was four years old and asked, "Why didn't you let me be born first? I was with you in San Francisco." Naturally, this was a major shock to her at the time.

My mother read extensively on spiritual topics through the years. Although her spiritual beliefs were grounded in Christianity, they also contained aspects of Eastern religions. Beliefs in reincarnation and karma—which can be summarized in the phrase "as ye sow, so shall ye reap"—are shared by much of the world's population, and by increasing numbers of Americans today as well. Mom believed the major reason for coming into this life is to learn, grow and evolve both personally and spiritually. This cannot be fully achieved in a single life span, so a soul decides what major lessons it will work on as it approaches each lifetime. This belief gave my mother the conviction that people have multiple opportunities to succeed in their inner and outer journey.

She recognized that there is always time, yet there is no time to waste.

Over the years, numerous people sought Mom out for spiritual guidance. She never accepted any money or gifts—the help she gave people was the only gift involved. At times she would read a person's cards. Her practice was similar to tarot but used 36 regular playing cards rather than a tarot deck. (Many people who are adept at tapping into unseen energy or knowledge say that it does not matter whether they use cards, a crystal ball, tea leaves or something else as an energy-focusing tool. If the person is gifted, the vehicle used makes little difference.) Mom read my cards on occasion beginning when I was a teenager. When I was in college, I occasionally brought home friends with whom I had shared spiritual discussions, and invariably they became interested in meeting my mother. Next, they often wanted to have their cards read, and my mother was always willing to oblige.

One of the extraordinary "readers" to whom Mom introduced me was named Elsie. I'm sorry to say I don't recall her last name. She lived in San Francisco, was in her mid-80s at this time, and was the most gifted psychic that I had experienced. I don't claim to understand her gift, nor can I explain it. I have only sought out such people two or three times and have generally been unimpressed, but Elsie convinced me. Today, I remain curious and try to keep an open mind.

Hearing Mom's extraordinary stories and her reflections on beliefs that were still far from the American mainstream, only three options were open to me. I could believe that she was foolishly gullible, that she was a pathological liar, or that she was a competent, sane and truthful person who had experienced events that were beyond conventional beliefs and understanding. Given those possibilities, there was really no choice. My mother was one of the sanest, most giving and most honest people I have ever known. She was also a hard-working survivor of loss with lots of common sense and shrewdness. If she believed that there was more to our lives than what could be proved or explained by traditional Western religion, I was willing to accept that as fact as well.

In addition to exemplifying spiritual depth and authenticity for me, my mother was an example of what it meant to be a strong, independent woman. In the Fifties and early Sixties, that wasn't the norm. She didn't raise me to fear female intelligence or demand female deference. I feel lucky to have been raised by a strong and amazing woman and then to meet another one very early in my dating years.

In the spring of 1965, when I was turning 20, I met MaryAnne Pramuk at a meeting of the Newman Club, a college-level Catholic youth organization. She was blonde and just short of five feet tall. Every bit of that five feet was gorgeous. She had an excellent brain, a beautiful smile, a great laugh and the personality to match. Her older brother, Joe, was my age; I knew him from our time together in the Boy Scouts years before, but by this time he was in college at University of San Francisco. MaryAnne's father was a physician and a veteran of the Korean War, during which he had served in a Mobile Army Surgical Hospital (MASH) unit. Later, he worked in the tuberculosis ward at Napa State Hospital, and he also gave the Boy Scouts physical exams before summer camp each year. I suppose I may have seen MaryAnne at her house when I went for those physicals.

But somehow she had changed between the ages of 13 and 18, and with those changes she got my complete attention.

The second of eight children, MaryAnne was raised in a devout Catholic home. MaryAnne's maternal grandmother had come to live with the family after the birth of their fourth child. There was lots of love and music in their household. MaryAnne's mom loved to cook and her dad taught the five brothers barbershop harmony after dinner around a large oval dining room table. (They still sing from time to time.) Gradually, I got to know—and grew to deeply appreciate—the loving, teasing, wonderfully humorous and very intelligent Pramuk "gang."

I don't think this was intentional, but MaryAnne had a sheltered upbringing with no introduction to any religious or philosophical views beyond those of the Catholic Church. She attended Catholic school from seventh grade through high school. She then drifted away from the Church, eventually realizing that she had questions about Church doctrine.

MaryAnne's first job was as a medical transcriptionist in the pathology department at Queen of the Valley Hospital in Napa. She took classes at Napa Junior College; later, after I was out of the army, she would continue with classes at Butte Community College and California State University at Chico. Over time, she became interested in the field of medical records. After working part time in the records department of a skilled nursing facility, she earned a degree as an accredited medical records technician and would consult and audit medical records in skilled nursing facilities around Northern California. But of course, in our early days together, all of that was still to come.

Not long after I started dating MaryAnne, I brought her home to meet my mother. They hit it off immediately. Before long they were having lengthy discussions about religion and spirituality. Topics included reincarnation and one of my mother's most cherished beliefs, the idea that Christ lay within each of us. Instead of worshiping a spiritual entity above us, Mom felt that each of us has within our soul all of the potential of the Christ and that each of us is evolving in that direction. For example, my mother believed that our mutual healings at the hands of David were the work of an advanced soul who is one with the ultimate spiritual source. In MaryAnne's view, my mother was an extraordinary woman: gentle, loving, and full of spiritual power. She treasured her time with Ruth. As happy as her own home was, MaryAnne appreciated the way her talks with my mother broadened her views and her feeling about what spirituality meant. Not just MaryAnne but several other members of her family as well had numerous conversations with Mom. All were deeply and positively affected by these spiritual discussions over time. Many found my mother's take on spiritual matters to be not only interesting, but also helpful in their own approach to spirituality.

4
IT'S ALL IN THE WRIST

By the year I turned 20, I had a budding romance with a soul mate. I also had that other essential for a young man, a car, and it was cars that introduced me to the man who would become a best friend.

Starting at the age of 15, in a period of five years I owned (in this order) a '50 Plymouth, a '49 Hudson, a '49 Mercury, a '52 Ford, a '57 Isetta 300, a '57 Plymouth, and a '62 Chevy II (later to be known as a Nova). I would drive up to our neighborhood gas station in whatever jalopy I owned at the time and ask for 75 cents worth of gas (or whatever amount I could spare from the change in my pocket). Of course, gas was only about 30 cents a gallon, and if I was lucky, two service stations near each other would be engaged in a price war that would bring the price even further down.

I was a regular customer at the Signal gas station down the street from our house. The owner's son, George Hewitt, worked for his dad and attended the junior college. While he put the gas in the car and washed the windshield, we would make small talk. Although he was only eight months older than me, he was two years ahead of me in school.

One day George suggested that we go on a double date. It turned out that his girlfriend was Sandie. I knew and liked her from high school and the better I got to know him, the more George seemed like an interesting guy. He was both bright and funny, one of my favorite combinations. When asked a question he frequently took time to consider it before responding, and his responses were well thought out. I tried to be thoughtful as well, so I appreciated his reflective approach to serious issues.

As we spent time at the gas station, at his house, or most often in his car or mine just cruising around, the topic of "the war" naturally came up. By the mid- to late Sixties, you didn't have to identify what war you were referring to. "The war" meant one thing: Vietnam.

The conflict had been in existence since 1950, but had only begun to loom large in the public consciousness in the 1960s. America's deepening involvement in Southeast Asia was an outgrowth of the Cold War, fueled by the government's fear of the spread of Communism from North Vietnam. By 1960, President Kennedy was determined to "draw a line in the sand" and prevent a communist victory in Vietnam. American involvement rapidly escalated under Lyndon Johnson, with a ground war added to the original aerial campaign. In 1965 alone, the Marine force on the ground grew from 3,500 to 200,000 Americans.

Suddenly, or so it seemed, Vietnam was front and center in American life. For some time, we saw the coffins of the fallen coming off the planes from Vietnam draped with American flags every night on the 6 p.m. news. Eventually the government banned the sharing of such footage; instead, a reporter would tell us how many Americans had died in the past week. Even after the coffins disappeared from public view, the news showed us scenes of Americans in battle gear moving through dense jungles and swamps, ready to engage the enemy at any moment. We learned that the North Vietnamese used guerilla warfare to great effect, and that any path could be set with deadly booby-traps.

Television and print reportage made it harder for many not to question our role in the conflict. Why were Americans dying for what was actually a civil war between communist North Vietnam and South Vietnam? Was the "domino theory," which held that if we lost Vietnam we might lose all of Southeast Asia to Communism, actually correct? For the first time in modern warfare, technology was bringing the actual scenes of war into living rooms throughout the country…and what it showed cast doubt on whether this war was necessary, winnable, or just. More and more Americans began to think twice.

America became a land divided between those who supported the government and the military and those who saw the conflict overseas as an unjust or at least unnecessary war. The split was to some degree generational. Older citizens—who had lived through World War II, been raised in a "my government right or wrong" mindset, and had never seen America lose a war—tended to support the military action. Many younger citizens—those who were being asked to fight the war and their peers—disagreed. They didn't understand the supposed threat, they saw Vietnam as a lost cause, and they questioned the justice of this war and war generally, with its seemingly never-ending carnage for no discernible reason. As well as questioning war, they questioned a government that seemed increasingly untrustworthy: fighting and killing for the wrong reasons, and manipulating citizens as well.

The original Selective Service Act, passed into law in 1917, permitted the U.S. government to conscript men for military service. Updated and reshaped by new legislation and executive orders over the decades, the Act required able young men between the ages of 18 and 25 (later stretched to age 35) to serve a minimum of two years on active duty by the time George and I began talking about the war. The conflict in Vietnam demanded a constant stream of fresh soldiers. The total number of young men drafted between 1964 and 1973 was reported to be 1,857,304, and a great many of them would be going to fight in the Vietnam War.

For those reluctant to take part in a war they didn't believe in, the alternatives were few. They could avoid it temporarily by attending college and getting a college deferment; they could get married and have a baby immediately; they could mutilate themselves in some way so as to be of no use to the military; they could give up their citizenship and emigrate to another country such as Canada, with no guarantee they could ever return; or they could refuse to serve and go to prison. Simply refusing to register for the draft could mean a prison term of up to five years and a fine of $50,000. In an age when military service is voluntary, it's hard to remember or imagine how these stark, even searing choices affected not only draft-eligible men but their loved ones and communities.

A battle raged not only halfway around the world in Vietnam but also in the hearts and minds of tens of thousands of Americans. Friendships, families and communities were split along increasingly intense and bitter lines, with beliefs that seemed totally irreconcilable. Almost everyone on both sides wanted to do the right thing, they just didn't agree on what the right thing was.

Being a student allowed me to defer my military service and the hard choices it would require. While working the night shift stocking shelves for a grocery, I attended Napa Community College, trying out a series of majors with no clear idea of a direction other than that of extracurricular and social activities. The only area of study that held my interest was psychology. But once I'd taken the school's only two psychology courses, I'd run out of options to pursue that further.

Academically, I did just enough to get by. This left my grade point average too low to enter a four-year college. So, as I started my third year at the community college in the fall of 1965, the local draft board started sending me form letters that asked when I might be leaving for a four-year institution. That was a signal to me that the fun and games were over and it was time to get to work. I got serious about my academics and started getting much better grades, all the while assuring the draft board that I would soon move on to the next academic level.

At the time I met George, I wasn't against the war. Though I felt confused by Vietnam, my mom's patriotism and respect for both the military and the responsibilities of American citizens still shaped many of my assumptions. But when I told George I was considering going into the Marine Corps after college, he looked at me as though I was out of my mind. George's parents had emigrated from Canada when he was eight years old. He had missed out on much of the patriotic and militaristic training that many kids in this country receive in their formative years. As he questioned me regarding my thoughts on Vietnam, it became clear that there was a whole lot that I didn't know or understand about this war. As time passed I began to question it, and my potential role in it, more seriously.

Over time, as I learned more about Vietnam, I dropped any aspirations regarding ROTC. It felt evident to me that regardless of my government's perspective, the arguments against the war were stronger than those in favor of it. I was now clear on the fact that I had no desire to take part in this war.

One afternoon my mother approached me and said, "Don, if you don't feel right about this war and your participation in it, you can ask in prayer to be spared that experience."

The odd thing about that was that I believed her, and yet for some reason I could never bring myself to ask to be spared.

I considered the possibility of identifying as a conscientious objector, but I knew that I really didn't qualify—it would have been a considerable reach if I'd tried. I didn't doubt that if an enemy landed on the coast of California, I would seek out a weapon and prepare to do battle. In good conscience, I just couldn't go with the conscientious objector option.

I also spent some time hitting the books...with my knee. Halfway through my freshman year I developed a bad bursitis on my right knee as a result of playing football for the junior college. My doctor told me that I was risking awakening every day for the rest of my life with pain in my leg if I continued playing. Not surprisingly, a year later this planted a thought in my head: if I could re-injure my knee, perhaps Uncle Sam would be less interested in me. It seems that hitting your knee with a heavy book does not have the same effect as being repeatedly smashed by a 200-pound lineman. Alas, my knee remained healthy despite the punishment, and I continued to be eligible to go to war. After this feeble attempt to maim myself, I accepted the fact that neither my body nor my mind was willing to do what it took to escape the war. Another option off the table.

At his house one day in the fall of 1965, George presented me with a strange request. He had previously broken a bone in his wrist while playing football for a college team. X-rays of this break had convinced the military to give him a 4F draft classification. He was quite pleased with that, as many a young lad would be when facing the Vietnam "police action." But it seems there was a problem.

"I went to my doctor yesterday, and x-rays showed that the bone in my wrist is mending," George told me.

Having charted his life path without any military detours, George had come to the conclusion that the most reasonable course of action would be to re-break his wrist, thereby ensuring his continued 4F status. The only question was how to get that accomplished. I was only mildly surprised to learn that he had a plan that included me. As we stood there in his parents' living room, he said, "I need you to help me re-break my wrist."

"Hold up, George. What are you talking about?" I said.

He said, "I figure if I hold my wrist just about like this and you hit it as hard as you can, that should do it."

The plan began with each of us drinking a couple of beers. It was about 11 o'clock in the morning, so luckily we had all day. Once we felt prepared we launched into Phase Two. This part of the plan required that he stand with his arm out and his wrist turned in just such a way that the bone might be broken again if struck with sufficient force. And, yes, I was to provide the sufficient force. I took a couple deep breaths while he turned his head away and closed his eyes. I'm not in the habit of trying to maim my friends, and the thought was, shall we say, disturbing at the very least.

"George, are you sure you want to do this?"

"Oh, yeah. I'm sure. Let's get it done."

Telling myself silently that I might be saving him from a more serious wound, I took careful aim and hauled off with a roundhouse swing, hitting his fist with my fist as hard as I could. I felt horrible as I watched him dance around the room grimacing in pain and cursing a blue streak. I felt horrible for having caused him such discomfort. I felt even worse because I knew that I had only hit him with a glancing blow, definitely not enough to accomplish a broken wrist. I started apologizing, thinking that we were done.

"Damn, George, I'm really sorry! I thought I had it lined up well. So much for that plan."

"You don't get outta here that easy, cowboy."

Clearly, George had other ideas. He suggested we drink another beer. Seemed like a reasonable idea to me. A few minutes later we tried the blow again. This time my aim was true, and my fist hit his with a loud pop. George once again danced around the room doing the "Damn that hurts" two-step. We parted company when the beer ran out.

When I saw him a week later, George was all smiles. He had been to his doctor for new x-rays. They showed that not only had we re-broken the wrist bone in question, we had broken yet another one. My friend George was thus 4F for the duration. Who knows, I may have saved his life…but I went home that night shaking my head at the craziness of it all.

5

DALY CITY—VISIBILITY ZERO

In the spring of 1966 I knew that my life as a civilian was continuing on borrowed time. I had applied for admission to San Francisco State College, but at the moment I still didn't have the grades to get in. I had dreams of being a psychologist and having a career in which I could help people with serious problems. At that time, San Francisco State, one of the many schools in the California State University system, had one of the largest psychology departments on the West Coast. Even beyond my hopes of avoiding the war, I was anxious to enroll there and explore the field of psychology further.

The folks at the draft board were breathing down my neck. I was busting my butt and doing extremely well in my classes at the junior college. It was the end of the semester and grades were due to come out very soon, but I decided to act. In my admission materials, I asked San Francisco State to wait for the current semester's grades. They sent me a letter of denial. I went to see the acting Dean of Men, Mrs. Murdoff, and pled my case. I knew I was getting mostly A's and perhaps one or two B's. The faculty had already turned in grades, so she went to the files to check on mine. She said, "You got a 3.7 this semester. Congratulations." Having done the math, I knew those grades would make me eligible for admission at San Francisco State. She and I went to see Tom MacMillan, a faculty member whom she knew was a San Francisco State graduate. He looked at the grades and got on the phone. Hanging up, he said, "You have an appointment tomorrow morning with the dean of admissions. You need to take a sealed copy of your grades to show him." My hopes were rising fast.

The next morning I walked into the San Francisco State admissions office. The dean there opened the sealed envelope, looked at the grades and said, "Congratulations. You've been admitted to San Francisco State." This meant that I would be able to finish my bachelor's degree before worrying further about the draft. You can't imagine my relief.

In the fall of 1966 George and I both escaped our long and dubious careers at Napa Junior College, but parted ways in the process. George was accepted at Chico State College and I was accepted at San Francisco State. Since the schools were only four hours apart, it was by no means an end to the relationship, just some temporary separation.

My mother and stepfather had limited funds, and my siblings—Mark, Paul and baby sister, Mary—were still at home. My parents' contribution to my college education was managed by borrowing enough to buy me a homemade 20-foot trailer that we towed to Daly City, not far from the San Francisco State campus. Parked in a small trailer park, its $35 a month rent was much cheaper than the dorms, and, since I was already a junior, this arrangement would only need to serve me for two years—with luck. It was a very workable plan as far as I was concerned, but it did take my parents a number of years to pay off that loan. I was very grateful for their sacrifice.

The move from Napa to San Francisco represented a major shift in my life. Going from a small community college in my hometown to a large state college in a big city took me from being a good-sized frog in a small pond to being a miniscule frog in a big pond. The adjustment was difficult, a truth that many a college student before me had already learned. I missed my friends and family and especially MaryAnne.

The late Sixties were complex times on college campuses. Sometimes the energy was creative and hopeful, sometimes contentious or dark. Students occupied college administration offices, turned out for large protests and sit-ins, and participated in draft-card burnings (which were serious illegal acts). In response, police and the National Guard were sometimes called out in an effort to control the crowds. The shooting of four Kent State students by the Ohio National Guard was still four years away when I arrived at San Francisco State, but the sense of volatility was already present on most campuses.

Another challenge for me was related to the issue of diversity. My hometown was a white vacuum, small and insulated. There never seemed to be more than one African American family living in town; rumor was that the real estate people made it difficult enough that African Americans soon gave up attempts to buy in the Napa Valley, a process called redlining. As a result, I grew up in an environment that was pretty much all white. By the time I moved to San Francisco State, I was hungry to meet people of different ethnicities, backgrounds and perspectives. But growing up in a small town with the same friends throughout life meant I had never really had to reach out to make new friends. Basically shy, I was inexperienced at and hesitant about reaching out to form new friendships. The few times that I got my courage up and reached out, it didn't work out well.

Underlying my own personal struggles was the racial unrest of the time. African Americans active in the Civil Rights Movement were demanding equal rights and asserting the need for black power through organizations from the NAACP to the Black Panthers. Much of the South, however, was still segregated, and African Americans were second-class citizens with limited rights. Peaceful "freedom marches" and sit-ins by blacks often resulted in violent clashes with local police, who used a variety of methods to both harass and intimidate protesters, including beatings, police dogs, and high-pressure fire hoses. Not that the police were responsible for all violence against blacks; in 1963, for example, an African American church in Atlanta was bombed by members of the Ku Klux Klan, resulting in the death of four young African American girls.

Later, I would understand better why my search for new friends sometimes met with anger, distrust or hostility on the part of people of color. But at the time, I would take my shy little white ass back to my trailer in Daly City, feeling sorry for myself and horribly misunderstood...even though a chunk of that misunderstanding was certainly my own.

The constant fog of Daly City added to my depressed mood.

It seemed that I would go for days without seeing the sun. I didn't know anyone in the trailer park and had little interest in making acquaintances there. I had not reached out to others in my classes either, so I was developing no new friends. I went through the motions during the week and did what I had to do to get by in my college classes, which as yet didn't include the more specialized courses in psychology that I most looked forward to. Listening to depressing music and writing bad poetry, I only came alive on weekends when MaryAnne would visit. Just knowing she was coming made my spirits soar.

By Christmas, I knew that I could not go on like this very much longer. I was realistic enough to understand that even MaryAnne could not solve all my problems. But I also knew with increasing certainty that she was the key to my happiness. On Christmas Eve 1966 I requested and received permission from her father to ask for her hand in marriage. (It might have been the "swingin' Sixties, but yes, I chose to go "old school.") That evening I took MaryAnne down to Napa's wonderfully green Fuller Park, seated her on a bench, bent onto one knee and proposed to her. My artistic mother had decorated a very small box to hold the ring. As part of the presentation I sang her an Elvis Presley song, "Loving You." To say MaryAnne was pleased would be a grave understatement. She seemed to be somewhere between thrilled and ecstatic.

When we returned to her parents' home to make the announcement, we found that the decorated Christmas tree had just fallen over and the house was in a tizzy. All in all, a memorable evening for just about everyone, if not entirely for the same reason.

MaryAnne's folks were not surprised when we broke the news, of course, since her dad had gotten prior warning. Nor were my mother and stepfather. Red, was a different story, since he was out on the road working. I wrote a letter telling him my plans. He had no idea that the relationship had become so serious. However, he didn't object.

Red was still sending me money each month. When I realized that I could squeak by on about half what he sent, I began saving the other half. It didn't occur to me at the time to check that with him, but today, I'm grateful that he was giving me enough to have this extra left over.) Now, I got the notion of doing something special for MaryAnne in the way of a honeymoon. It was a plan that worked to perfection. We made our plans for an August wedding.

6

LIFE AT THE MINI-RANCH

In the summer of 1967, my beloved MaryAnne and I were married on the hottest day of the year. The night before, my buddies had thrown a bachelor party that finally ended up at the local pancake house. Despite the fact that I was probably the soberest person in the group, my friends had conspired to have a local policeman take me downtown and put me in the drunk tank. They left me there for about an hour. When I was released they were all there at the station house yukking it up. I suppose you can only get away with something like this in a small town like Napa was in 1967.

The wedding came off with only a small hitch or two and the ceremony was as lovely as one can expect at a temperature of 99 degrees. MaryAnne was the most beautiful bride I had ever seen. Her smile lit up the entire church. She took my breath away! When the priest said, "You may kiss the bride," there wasn't a moment's hesitation. I felt like the luckiest guy in the world.

At the reception, the baker delivered us a hideous dark blue cake. I am told he stopped the bride and groom at the other wedding just before they were to cut into our lovely cake. Switching the cakes in the nick of time, the baker brought our own cake back to our hungry guests. Aside from the cake snafu, the fact that the band was pretty much a total loss, and the fact that the photographer had no idea what he was doing, it was a good bash.

On the day of our wedding, MaryAnne was 20 years old and I was 22. Like so many, we probably married for all the wrong reasons, but we were young and in love and that was all the reason we needed. She was looking for a big strong guy to take care of her. I was looking for a lovely young lass to take care of. Later, as she grew to want a more 50-50 relationship, I was growing in the direction of wanting the same. Needless to say, this worked out rather well. We were lucky to have a marriage that grew even stronger as time passed. Many friends weren't so lucky, and later rued their youthful choices of mate.

I had convinced MaryAnne we were honeymooning in Disneyland, and she was a good sport about it. Her brother Joe aided in the deception and so, unwittingly, did the much more minimal airport signage and announcements of the time. Today, it would be hard to get someone on a plane without them knowing its destination, but it was possible back then. When our stewardess began demonstrating proper use of the life vests, MaryAnne asked, "Why is she doing that if we're only going to Disneyland?" I responded, "Well, sometimes they have to fly out over the ocean to line up for the landing." Shortly thereafter, our stewardess announced our destination as Hawaii. Even then, MaryAnne thought we were on the wrong plane. Only when she saw the smile on my face did she realize the truth.

As advertised, Honolulu was lush and beautiful. MaryAnne thought she was in a dream. The hotel was a couple blocks from Waikiki Beach, and we arrived at about 10 o'clock in the beautiful, warm starry night. The kind fellow behind the desk realized that we were newlyweds and rather than checking us into the more modest room I had booked on my budget, gave us the bridal suite on the top floor for the evening since it wasn't booked. Hawaiian music was playing softly in the background; the air was filled with the aroma of beautiful flowers; the suite was lovely. The evening was perfect, and we were truly in heaven.

We rented a car the next day so we could get around the island. We did all the normal "touristy" stuff and enjoyed the beach almost daily. The second week we were there, George and Sandie, who he had recently married, came to Honolulu as well. We met downtown and surprised Sandie, who didn't know that MaryAnne and I had passed on Disneyland. My new bride and I hung out with our friends some, but most of the time the two of us were on our own, which suited us just fine.

We had a blowout dinner at the Colony Surf on Waikiki to celebrate our first "weekly-versary." The chateaubriand at the wonderful restaurant, right on the beach, was perfect. We were the last people in the restaurant that night. I left $50 on the table to pay the bill and give our waiter a nice tip. In 1967, that was an expensive dinner. The two weeks flew by. We savored every moment. We got home to Napa with a total of $44 to begin our marriage.

We had initially planned on living in the trailer in Daly

City, but an opportunity arose to rent a small cottage just outside Napa for the ridiculously low price of $35 a month, the same cost as the lot rental for the trailer. We hauled the trailer from Daly City up to Napa and parked it behind the cottage, which was surrounded by open fields and a few redwoods. We had only one neighbor and they had only one pet, a peacock that would serenade us frequently. As I've said, we called the place the "mini-ranch" and we loved it.

We had already purchased a large couch that folded out to make a bed. Now we used it in the cottage, in what was the living room by day and the bedroom by night. We had brought home the straw mats that we had used on the beach in Honolulu. They worked well as window shades. The kitchen in the cottage was so small that to enter the kitchen, we had to turn sideways to get past the refrigerator; when we bent down to look in the oven, our rear ends went in the garbage container. But in the end, it mattered little. We were in love and would have lived in a cardboard box.

MaryAnne was working at the local hospital as a medical transcriber for a pathologist, and I was stocking shelves on the night crew at a local supermarket. I pretty much worked my way through college as a part-time grocery clerk at Safeway and other stores. The swing shift from 3 p.m. to midnight worked well for me. I could usually get along on about five hours sleep.

I had long been wanting a dog, and the mini-ranch was a perfect place, with room for a dog to run in whatever direction she chose. An ad in the newspaper led us to Anna. She was a full-blooded German shepherd with papers and a strong bloodline. When we took her for dog training, the

MaryAnne and I, 1966

The "Mini-Ranch," 1967

instructor said that Anna was very smart and we would have to work hard to stay one step ahead of her. Another soul to share our house.

In my senior year of college, 1967-68, I commuted the 50 or so miles from the mini-ranch to San Francisco State for classes three days a week. (I had been able to get the classes I needed on Monday, Wednesday and Friday.) As I mentioned earlier, college campuses were alive with protests and San Francisco State was no exception. There seemed to be a special energy in the air, as though something unexpected could happen at any moment. The Governor, Ronald Reagan, had replaced college president Dr. Summerskill with Dr. S.I. Hayakawa. Hayakawa was a hardliner when it came to protests. At times I would walk across the campus and watch the clash between protesters and police. I watched but I didn't take part. It seemed as though some officers enjoyed the confrontations. Some police carried nightsticks, really clubs, of white oak; some of the nightsticks were left visibly bloodstained, as though that was some badge of honor. It was still not clear to me whether our part in the war was justified. I didn't know who to believe; I only knew that I had no desire to take part in a divisive war that seemed to be tearing our country apart.

I was trying to figure out the nature of the cosmos and my place in it. I had stopped going to Mass or taking part in any Catholic activities when I moved out of my parents' house. I still believed in the broader spiritual teachings I had learned from my mother, so you might say I was on a spiritual search to understand those teachings better.

Early in my marriage, my mother encouraged me to take

up meditation. One night, after some weeks of meditation practice in the darkened bedroom, my mind took a surprising turn. In my mind's eye I saw our dog standing in the doorway with her back to me, retching as though she were sick and vomiting. My immediate reaction there in the silent darkness was to scold myself for letting my mind wander. I knew she was under the bed. I told myself, "Come on, now, get back to meditation. Get a grip."

In the dark, I could hear Anna scrambling to get out from under the bed, and then I heard the same retching sounds I had imagined a minute before. When I reached over and turned on the light, there was Anna standing in the doorway with her back to me, vomiting. What was actually happening was identical to the picture I had seen in my mind. This experience shocked me, to say the least. Seeing something before it actually happened was spooky. I was alarmed as well as curious. Much to my later regret, I stopped meditating at that point. At some level it must have really frightened me. MaryAnne said that for her, the incident was evidence that premonitions are possible. But she also understood my alarm.

It was at this time that I met Michael, another "psych" student at SF State, with whom I shared a couple classes. He had the look of a full-on hippie, hardly unusual at that time. About five feet nine inches tall, he had a bushy head of black curly hair, wire-rimmed glasses, and a good deal of energy. Michael was intelligent, well spoken, and quite artful at cutting corners when it came to class assignments. But he had a personal style about him that intrigued me.

After we had known each other for a few weeks, he turned me on to a man called Alex, who had a following of largely college-age people. It was difficult to characterize the variety of people who came to hear Alex talk. I listened to Alex speak on spiritual issues one day and was most definitely intrigued. I'm embarrassed to say that after all these years I can't even remember what it was that intrigued me. Having seen my mother thrive thanks to David's presence in her life, I may have been hoping Alex was a similarly powerful figure.

At a previous meeting, Alex's audience had been a mixture of folks ranging from hippies to "straights." It hadn't seemed threatening or odd. When MaryAnne and I were invited to a gathering one weekend, I told her I wanted to go.

MaryAnne said, "It's probably going to be a bunch of people dancing around the bonfire naked."

I laughed. "No, I don't think so. I would really like to see what this fellow has to offer. Will you come? If it's not good, we can leave."

She responded, "Okay, we'll see what he has to say."

Following the directions given, we eventually arrived at a small ranch property near the Marin coast. It was dark and I couldn't be sure just what we were approaching, but we pressed on. In the end it turned out MaryAnne was right about the bonfire and the nudity! I felt a bit foolish. She didn't let me live that one down for some time. That was the late Sixties, and as the decade's famous anthem, "San Francisco," said, those heading for San Francisco needed to wear some flowers in their hair. Other than that, apparently, dress was optional.

7

OH CANADA

I received my bachelor's degree from San Francisco State in June 1968. I had been going to one form of school or another since day care at the age of three. That added up to about 20 years of school. I didn't even go through the graduation ceremonies, telling myself that I would do that when I got my master's. It felt as though I was far from done. I knew I would have to gain another degree before I could expect much in the way of job opportunities. It quickly became apparent to me that the best job I could find with my new bachelor's degree in hand was that of probation officer. While that's a noble profession, it held no interest for me. I was now applying for master's degree programs in the field of psychology, hoping the war would end or something else would intervene.

It was precisely at this period that President Lyndon Baines Johnson did away with graduate school draft deferments. I assume they must have needed more draft-eligible young men to fight the war. Anyone already well along in a master's program could continue to defer the draft. But those who had just—or not yet—started were out of luck. Virtually the entire male college graduating class of 1968, excepting those who were deemed medically unfit or were married with children, was now eligible to be drafted, and many were. Timing is everything, and right then it didn't work in my favor.

In the meantime, in the summer of 1968 I was looking for a job. Cork Kennedy, a close friend, was in a similar quandary as to how to approach being drafted. He and I had met while we were both going to the junior college. We both served in positions on the college's board of student commissioners. I had been on a fraternity flag-football team, and he was one of the referees. We had hit it off pretty well, and he was a frequent visitor to the mini-ranch. He was a trivia buff, an expert on Broadway musicals and a very entertaining guest. He was a year older than me and therefore even more draft eligible. He was considering the possibility of conscientious objector status but was dubious that he could qualify.

With the draft now hanging over my head and my student deferment gone with the stroke of Johnson's pen, my options were narrowing rapidly. It seemed to me that I had three alternatives: I could go to prison (not desirable); I could head for Canada (lots of questions); or I could simply accept the fate that lay before me.

On the other hand, the recently broken-wristed George had no such worries. After all, he was 4F. The owner of a Mini Cooper S, George wanted to go to the state of Washington that summer to compete in a road race. He asked me to come along and navigate. I told him I would come along if, after the race, we could head north into British Columbia, where I could test the waters of moving to Canada to see how doable it might be. That evening I brought up the topic of the sojourn into Canada with MaryAnne. While she wasn't thrilled about me going, she didn't argue or try to talk me out of it. She understood the importance of this trip and was willing to move to Canada if that was what was necessary. She felt the same desperation that I did. My going off to war was about the worst thing she could think of. The relative disadvantages of being drafted versus immigrating to Canada were much discussed at the mini-ranch during this time—as I've said, we never did move into the house on Cherry Street, so the mini-ranch remained home base for quite a while.

For those who didn't live through the years of the Vietnam conflict, I should add that leaving the U.S. to avoid the draft was a crime. Those who tried to return (even temporarily, to visit friends or family) faced imprisonment or forced military service. No one in 1968 would have bet on the pardon that President Carter offered draft evaders in 1977, one day after he took office. For all those reasons, going to Canada wasn't a temporary strategy. If you went, you had to do so knowing you might never be able to see your home again.

George agreed to the side trip to British Columbia, so when the time came, we set off. The road race took us through some of the countless forests of Washington State, which required our full attention as we slid around blind corners and sped down occasional straightaways with the pedal to the metal. As navigator, my job was to ensure that we were following the race route correctly and not taking any wrong turns. It was great fun. Each car set off individually and was timed as to how long it took to complete the course. George, a good driver, did quite well—we ended up in the top 10 within our automotive group. Engaging as it was, when we were not racing, my mind was on Canada's possible role in my future.

After the two-day race, we headed north as agreed. I was both anxious and curious as we set off. All in all, I was seeing a bit of hope. It was summer, and the forested landscape was magnificent, with an all-encompassing scent of pine that was truly invigorating. The weather was good and our spirits were high. However, having limited cash, economy was foremost on our minds.

As we approached the border, the fact that we were about to enter another country became more real. Now really focusing on the possibility of moving beyond the U.S., I found my mind racing with questions. What kind of job could I get? What kind of a budget would we live on? I wondered what type of housing would be available and what part of Canada we might live in. Probably British Columbia, but that covers a lot of ground. What would it be like to live in the snow several months each year? Without friends and family nearby, how difficult would it be to make new friendships? If we lived in Canada, would we ever be able to return? The answers to such questions were cloudy. Passing through the border control was simple and straightforward, but everything else felt unclear and without guarantees.

We continued north with the city of Victoria as our ultimate target. Along the way, we made a stop at Simon Fraser University in Vancouver. I knew I wanted to attend graduate school, and this was a chance to see a prestigious Canadian university firsthand. Exploring the campus, we found the people friendly and helpful as we asked for directions and information. In time, we reached the psychology department and gathered information regarding their programs.

Though the questions at hand were grave, there were some funny moments. As we continued our self-guided tour of the campus, I needed to use the restroom. When I tried to open the door of the stall I was in, the latch was broken. Despite my repeated attempts to open it, the door remained locked. No matter what I did, I couldn't get the door to budge. My frustration growing, I considered kicking the door down, but thought better of it. I took a deep breath as I considered my options. I could get down on my belly and crawl out of the stall or I could choose the high road (literally), climbing up and over the door to make my escape from what was beginning to feel more like a cell than a stall. Surveying the less than immaculate condition of the floor, I opted to climb up and over.

I began my climb. Don't ask me how, but in the process of scaling over the door I managed to get my pants caught on the hook fastened to the inside of it. At that point I heard a loud ripping sound and instantly knew I was in big trouble. In my effort to free myself, I had torn the rear end out of my pants. Now free of the stall, I stood there in a state of panic and disbelief. George stifled a laugh but could not stop himself from making smartass remarks. After a couple minutes of flustered hesitation, it became clear that I had little choice but to walk down the hall holding the rear of my pants closed as firmly as possible in an effort not to offend passersby. George and I sheepishly sought help in the closest room, where the office personnel did their best to avoid laughing out loud. We decided that of our limited options, the best temporary fix for my embarrassing condition was to borrow a stapler. We then attempted repairs as best we could, with George trying to mend the rip while trying not to staple me in the process. At that point our visit to Simon Fraser University came to an abrupt close, leaving the university with an indelible first impression of me and leaving me with little other than a ripping good tale.

We continued to drive north. To conserve cash, we left the car on the mainland and took a ferry to Nanaimo, a city on the east coast of Vancouver Island. The ferry ride was fun, and it was great being on the water. Then we hitchhiked down to Victoria. We caught a ride within about 15 minutes and the driver was kind enough to drop us off right downtown. Victoria is a beautiful historic city about 100 miles south of Nanaimo, on the southern end of Vancouver Island. The architecture of a time gone by was magnificent, and, the city being coastal, the water and the boats added further to its beauty.

We stayed a couple days checking out groups providing support to Americans coming to Canada, such as Cool-Aid and Friends of American War Resisters. These were loose-knit organizations made up largely of young people who had strong feelings against the war and who went out of their way to help those men coming from the United States to avoid the draft. They were willing to help those fleeing the draft by sharing food and floor space for sleeping while those young Americans were trying to get their feet under them.

Yes, it was clear to me that we could make the transition. But life would be somewhat more difficult than in the U.S. College tuition would cost more and pay for part-time work would not be comparable. I was used to being a journeyman clerk in the retail clerks' union within the Bay Area. In Canada, I would likely be paid about half of the salary I was making in California. I had no idea how difficult it might be to gain admission to a master's program in Canada. But what gave me most pause, of course, were other things—losing my identity as an American, moving away from every place with which I was familiar, leaving friends and family behind. For the moment, I didn't really face any of those big issues head on. But it was clear to me that such a move would result in a significant emotional adjustment for MaryAnne and myself, even though I couldn't really fathom the extent of it at that time.

George and I eventually felt we had learned all we could. Our funds running low, we returned to our car and started heading for home. We had not yet left Canada and were heavy into conversation when the car ahead of us suddenly stopped. We could not avoid a rear-end collision. George called the local State Farm insurance office and John, the insurance agent who came to help us, realized that we had little money left and no place to stay. He offered to put us up in his own house. We were dumbfounded by his generous offer, which meant hosting us for several days while the car was being repaired. We couldn't believe our good fortune. Nor were we in a position to turn such an offer down.

John took us in and treated us like visiting houseguests. I called MaryAnne to let her know what had happened. She was relieved to hear from me but naturally disappointed in the delay. John turned out to be a really nice guy, as one might surmise. He was a hard-working father of two teenage daughters and husband to a lovely lady named Sylvia. They were a delightful couple with whom we enjoyed a number of conversations regarding conditions in the United States and Canada. When Friday night came, we all went to a local beer garden and had a great evening. We were John's guests, and he wouldn't let us pay for anything. George's birthday fell during our stay with John and Sylvia. She actually went to the trouble of making him a cake. Pretty amazing. Clearly, I didn't need to fear that the people of Canada were not warm and welcoming.

We were waiting for the car to be repaired when one morning I found myself standing in a hillside parking lot, looking south—back toward the U.S.—over a large expanse of forest. George was in the shop watching them work on his car, so I was alone with my thoughts. As I stood there, the realities of this action were becoming clearer in my mind. This would not be a ho-hum move across country. It would bring with it long-term separations from family and friends. MaryAnne's family was such a tight-knit and caring group, I knew she would have a very difficult time and miss them terribly. How could I do that to her? The idea of losing touch with my own family caused another stab of pain. We would be transforming close relationships into long-distance ones and living without the knowledge of when, if ever, we might reunite. I wasn't thinking about children yet, but I had always expected that MaryAnne and I would have a family. Going to Canada would mean depriving us and our children of our families' emotional support. All of these were sobering thoughts.

Unexpectedly, I also faced the realization of how hard it would be to give up my American citizenship. MaryAnne and I would be something akin to fugitives and strangers in unfamiliar territory. It would mean changing our citizenship to Canadian and the likelihood of never being able to return to the United States legally. Suddenly I saw that my American identity, which I had taken for granted, was central to who I was.

I had clearly been avoiding these thoughts ever since we entered Canada. Now they hit me hard. My heart sank as I watched Canada become another untenable option for avoiding the war.

Once the car was repaired, we set off back to California. George was hurting because of the repair bill he had to pay. I was hurting because the Canadian option had been crushed.

The battle within me continued.

8

DRAFTED ON ELECTION DAY

When I arrived home, MaryAnne was naturally anxious to hear about Canada and what I had learned there. She had worked hard to adopt a positive attitude toward the move during my absence. It was a letdown of sorts for her to hear that I no longer saw Canada as an acceptable solution. It wasn't that she wanted to go to Canada—far from it. It was just that she liked the remaining options even less.

So, back at home, I denied the reality of the coming draft while deep down knowing that it would take a miracle to avoid military service. George and I had both been accepted to the Chico State master's program in psychology, and we celebrated with a few cold beers in the California sunshine. The summer of 1968 was sliding by, and I daily donned my rose-colored glasses. You have by now some notion of the gravity of the choices I faced. The metaphorical train I was on was actually headed toward one of three tracks: one led to a more serious attempt at maiming myself to make myself ineligible for military service; one led to a prison term if I refused to join the military; and one was headed ultimately to war. None of those trips held any promise. MaryAnne was just as desperate to ignore reality as I was. She was riding the fantasy line with me, and our tickets were punched for Chico and graduate school.

Now we're caught up to where I began this book. MaryAnne and I had rented a small house in Chico at something-and-a-half Cherry Street and I had gone through a bit of a mishap totaling my in-laws' automobile while taking the first load of our belongings there. The worst I got out of that accident was an injured right eardrum, but of course, adding insult to injury, Uncle Sam delivered me a draft notice on the same day as the car accident. I probably ought to mention that, right or wrong, I did try to capitalize on that ruptured eardrum once the doctor told me it was healing. Not knowing much about ruptured eardrums, I probably went about keeping it broken all wrong.

First, I fired off a .38 caliber pistol next to my ear— the handgun Red had given me as a college graduation present. (Go figure. Nothing says "Congratulations" like a gun.) Then I dove to the bottom of a swimming pool, hoping the pressure would do something. Finally, in a last-ditch effort, I went flying with a pilot who did a number of dives trying to help me out. None of those things worked, and I discovered that there was a limit as to how far I would go to maim myself. For instance, I heard about guys who blew off their trigger fingers, but the army would probably teach me to use another finger to pull the trigger. (Besides, that would definitely damage my typing skills.)

So in the end I followed through on my surrender to the draft board and showed up at the appointed time and place in downtown Napa. The bus would take me to the induction center, after which the Army would provide for all my needs.

There was naturally a sad and tearful goodbye with various family members but especially with MaryAnne. I tried to tell her that a bright and talented guy like me would probably end up behind a desk somewhere, but it didn't help. As I reassured her that I would be home on leave before long, she had me in a bear hug and didn't want to let me go. Eventually, it was last call and I had to get on the army transport bus.

I was nervous and in a lousy mood as I got on, but I found my buddy Cork Kennedy and another friend, Pete Langenbach, already on board. Pete and I were in the same graduating class. We had never been close friends; our relationship was the kind that forms when you play football with someone for a few years. I guess we would say we respected and liked each other. He had a stocky build and a tough look about him. The look didn't lie. You don't play first-string center on a football team if you're a wimp. Cork had an undergraduate degree in radio and television from San Francisco State, and Pete had a teaching credential from the same school. As I've mentioned, Cork was usually cheerful, but on this day his manner was not nearly so jovial. He was in no mood to entertain.

The bus took us to the Oakland induction center, where we would go through the ritual of being sworn into the United States Army. Here it was, the moment of truth, the moment I had been dreading. Thoughts flew through my mind, including all the machinations I had been through over the past five years as I avoided the draft. I had long since surrendered to the inevitability of this moment. The battle within my mind was now over and there was nothing more to do but step forward, say the words, and face whatever would come.

They lined us all up, told us to take one step forward and raise our hands, read us the oath, and then had us repeat it. Ironically enough, it was that very same day that Richard M. Nixon was elected the 37th President of the United States. I asked one of the sergeants if we would get a chance to vote. His answer was a flat "No." We were heading off to fight for our country, but our government had no interest in giving us a voice. Our anger made no difference to those in charge, a sign of things to come. Of course, I should have arisen early and gone to my polling place prior to the bus, but I guess I had other things on my mind that morning.

The swearing-in was followed by a bewildering wander through the complex as we were given a variety of inspections and injections. The place was idiot-proof. They had colored lines painted on the floor. All they had to do was tell you, "Follow the green line" and you'd go where you needed to get next.

We were then driven to the airport, where we were put on a plane headed to Seattle/Tacoma Airport. From there, we were taken to Fort Lewis, Washington. The base at Fort Lewis seemed to be standard army issue, pretty much as I had imagined it from movies and TV. Most buildings were of the same architectural style, two stories or less, nothing fancy but with lots of open space that offered plenty of room for marching and formation, the latter word military-speak for nice neat rows and columns of men. We seemed to have arrived in a well-groomed world. The vehicles were mostly military issue, all painted the same olive drab. The drill sergeants who yelled out orders looked pretty spiffy in their starched and ironed uniforms, shoes brilliantly ashine, hair closely cropped and everything in place.

One of the company's two platoons (less than the usual four) was made up of young men who had volunteered for military duty. They were termed Regular Army, or RAs. The other platoon was made up of draftees termed "U.S." Since President Johnson had recently done away with graduate school deferments, there were numerous soldiers who had a couple years of college if not a college degree. I think it was a shock to the drill sergeants. I could almost see what they were thinking: *Where did all these college-educated know-it-all's come from? Can we send them back?*

9

GETTING DOWN TO BASICS

Upon arrival at Fort Lewis, we were led to temporary barracks. Each barracks was a long rectangular building with two lines of bunk beds running its length. At the back on the ground floor were the latrine and showers. This would be our home for the next 10 days as we underwent what the army referred to as "orientation." We would be issued our uniforms, learn to march as a unit, get GI haircuts, labor insanely to acquire an appetite for military cuisine, and be taught what the army felt was necessary for us to know and do in order to begin basic training properly. It was after those 10 days that we were separated into two basic training companies and I had to bid a farewell to both Cork and Pete.

I assume my bachelor's degree in psychology is the reason I was asked to be a squad leader, an offer I accepted. I didn't mind taking that responsibility in a training situation but leading men into battle wasn't something I desired given that I had been put here against my will. Later on, when they asked me to go to officer candidate school, I said, "Thanks, but no thanks."

My squad included many college graduates in such fields as business, psychology, sociology, political science and chemistry. Jarrold Brown, the chemistry major, had a master's degree and was teaching high school chemistry when he was drafted. Short of stature and slightly built, his horn-rimmed glasses gave him a bit of a nerdy look that fit his personality well. He was highly intelligent, and I liked him right off the bat. Walter had recently taken the bar exam for South Dakota and was awaiting his results. Mixed into the group were a couple Idaho farm boys. These were good guys, and sharp ones too. But my, were they big.

Another notable person was Earl, a strange fellow who informed me, "Tonight would be a good night for a wolf hunt." Clearly, this was a group of recruits the likes of which 19-year-old drill sergeants had never encountered. When given an order, this group wanted to understand the reasoning behind it and had the infuriating habit of asking why. When told how to accomplish a task, they were likely to look at it and come up with a strategy that was different and, in their minds at least, generally superior to the army way. This tended to drive drill sergeants a little crazy.

Another fellow with whom I established a good relationship was Ron Principe. The gregarious Ron had a business degree from Sacramento State College. Slightly overweight and with an olive complexion suggesting his Mediterranean heritage, Ron was an expert at looking for an angle—any angle. And he frequently found one. He had a receding hairline, sharp facial features and piercing dark eyes. You could tell immediately that this was someone with an eye out for any way to avoid obstacles and achieve goals.

Jarrold, the diminutive and clever chemistry teacher, acted as a good counterweight for Ron, with his constant pessimism vying against Ron's overactive optimism. These two were to become my good friends and confidants as we faced the ups and downs of basic training in the snow of Washington State.

Nobody wants a lengthy description of basic training. It was rigorous, with plenty of physical exercise and considerably less sleep time than my system would have preferred. To quite a number in my platoon, all of the mandatory exertion proved very challenging. Many of the college graduates, being between 22 and 26, had not done serious physical exercise since they were 18 and graduating from high school. Five years of relative inactivity can take its toll, and some of these guys were really out of shape. I wasn't in the best condition myself. But the army has a program precisely designed to rectify this sort of problem. And rectify it they did. That's why the army has drill sergeants. They are the rectifiers.

Then there is the marching, less intense but more precise than the army's other forms of exercise. It is also the primary form of transportation for army recruits. Double-time marching has the advantage of getting you where you're going twice as fast but twice as worn out. Drill sergeants enjoy seeing recruits reach a destination twice as fast. It means that we have saved time, which can now be applied to another activity. Often that activity is called "Hurry up and wait."

Classroom lectures on a wide variety of military topics were also part of the program. Just when you were about to fall asleep while trying to maintain your attention, it was time to shift to an outdoor activity, such as shooting rifles, teargas training, or bayonet usage (which you were expected to accomplish without causing harm to yourself or your fellow recruits). When all else fails there were always assorted spit and polish exercises. Between the mud and the snow, it was an ongoing battle to keep my boots polished for surprise inspections. Some days were rainy and some were just plain cold, and then there was the snow.

All this effort took place in the midst of a miserable Washington winter. It was a surreal experience to practice low crawling (on your belly with a rifle) through several inches of snow while trying to imagine yourself in a tropical jungle

Fort Lewis, Washington, 1969

in Southeast Asia. I suppose it was natural in such circumstances for the mind to seek escape from the reality of the moment.

The best escapes took the form of letters and care packages from home. We savored the letters, reading them over and over. The handwriting on the letter was a sure tipoff as to whom it was from. You could get all the latest news from home plus lots of heartfelt feelings. Of course, you were always a little behind because, like sending a message to a far-off planet, the news always took a few days to get to you. It could get a little tricky if you each were expressing thoughts about an issue and the letters crossed in the mail. But, eventually, you and your correspondent would work it out. MaryAnne and I wrote almost daily and I treasured her every word.

Even guys without sweethearts craved letters. This was years before computers, the Internet and email. Cell phones were decades away. During basic, and then later during advanced training you could line up with the rest of the guys for the use of the public pay phone and hope that the person you wanted to talk to was there when you called. But for reliable communications, paper and pencil was your best bet.

The contents of the care packages I got would be gone immediately unless I could keep from giving in to my envious bunkmates. My packages often contained cookies, candy and a variety of salty snacks like crackers and nuts. Sometimes they included baked goods wrapped like little treasures trying to avoid breakage. Even though they were a week old on arrival and didn't travel very well, that never stopped us from enjoying them. Once in a while you might even get an item or two of canned goods such as fruit. On Valentine's Day MaryAnne cut out cookies in the shape of letters so the cookies spelled out "I love you."

My other escape took place after lights out, when I would pull my blanket over my head and read my paperback copy of the first book of the *Lord of the Rings* trilogy with a small flashlight. My plan was to nurse that first book through basic, the second book through advanced infantry training and the third through Vietnam. I was already a long way from The Shire and sure that I was destined to be "in the land of Mordor where the Shadows lie."

When I ran into Pete after a week or so, he told me that Cork was having a difficult time. This was no great surprise, since Cork was generally smarter than anyone he had ever worked under and he definitely had problems with many authority figures. I think he had a habit of pointing out failures, misjudgments, and errors others made. Judging that it was just a matter of time before things would blow up, I was quite worried about him.

I received no significant complaints regarding my job as squad leader, except for the time I forgot my rifle as I left a training exercise. In response, a drill sergeant was kind enough to instruct me on an hour's worth of push-ups, leg lifts and assorted calisthenics, as well as a strenuous bit of exercise referred to as the dying cockroach because that's what it most closely resembled. It wasn't fun, but I deserved what I got. Leaving my weapon behind was a very serious error.

At one point a couple weeks into training, it seemed like the guys in my squad were wound pretty tight. They seemed on edge and were sniping at each other. The frequency and gusto of laughter were diminishing. I was looking for a way to let them blow off some steam.

After some thinking, I walked from one end of the barracks to the other complaining about my squad's inability to make a good bunk. I tore portions of the bunks apart as I walked by. This was not going over well. The men spent a lot of time making their bunks just so, and if looks could kill, the undertaker would already be on the way to pick up my body. After I had messed up the last bunk, I turned to them and said, "What day of the week is it?" Someone said Wednesday, and I asked, "What do you do to your bunk tomorrow morning?" Then I started to see scowls turn into smiles. Thursday mornings, sheets went to the laundry; since it was 9 o'clock on Wednesday night, no one was going to be inspecting their beds before they had to remake them the next day. Howls went up as the squad members began to tear apart their buddies' beds, soon echoed by the other squad as they began to tear theirs up, too. It felt good to see the men finally show some signs of easing up. This became a Wednesday night ritual.

By the third week, training in the rain, snow and mud of the Washington winter was beginning to take its toll. Oddly enough, the men of the draftee platoon were holding up admirably while morning formations of the RA platoon were depleted by the numerous recruits reporting to sick call. I must admit that the men in the draftee platoon took a certain amount of pleasure in the fact that they were holding up better than the youngsters in this severe winter clime.

It was right at this time that I ran into Pete again. He told me, "Cork is in the brig. We got to that point in training where they wanted him to stab a bayonet into a dummy and yell, "Kill!" but he refused."

"What happened then?" I asked.

"They gave him a couple more chances, but he wouldn't budge."

This may seem to be a perfectly normal difference of opinion in the everyday world. But refusing to obey a direct order by a superior is, of course, something the United States Army cannot tolerate. It looked as though Cork was headed for a court-martial. I knew that once he had made up his mind the army would not be able to change it. I felt worried, sad and powerless to help him. At this point I pretty much lost contact with Cork, not connecting with him again for some months. Later, I learned that those running the brig realized that he was quite bright and could type. They made good use of his skills while he was with them. Even later, I discovered that Cork had been given a second court-martial. This time he had been sentenced to five years' imprisonment. Eventually given a bad conduct discharge, he was spared the five-year sentence by a stroke of unanticipated luck. Instead of being sent to Ft. Leavenworth as intended, his paperwork for discharge reached Ft. Lewis first. Just like that, he was a free man and on his way home. All of this I learned well after the fact, but even belatedly, I was glad to know that he was okay.

The year's end was approaching. Rumor had it we were going to get leave during the Christmas holidays. I was, naturally, very excited. When the time came, I found myself on a train headed for California along with a goodly number of other California GIs. Most of us had not seen liquor of any sort since being drafted, and the train had a bar that didn't ask for IDs. So we drank the train dry before we got out of Oregon. The railroad company must have been quite familiar with this kind of situation. They didn't stock enough alcohol in the bar to create serious problems, just enough to get our spirits up, and our spirits were pretty high to begin with. A few guys got kind of silly, but that was the extent of it. What with numerous stops along the way, it was an overnight trip, but I didn't sleep much sitting upright. Each stop along the way, often very long stops indeed, only served to prolong the ride and delay my eventual arrival home.

When we finally pulled into the station, I already had my bag in my hand. A very large part of me wanted to barge through the fellows in front of me, but, of course, that wasn't going to happen. When I spotted MaryAnne as I stepped off the train, my first thought was, "Good God! She's even more beautiful than I remembered!" After a good deal of kissing and hugging and laughing, I managed to stop long enough to greet Red as well. I wasn't surprised to see him. His job called for him to be in from the road at that time, and he had been more in touch since he realized I might be going to war. We then headed for Napa to see the rest of both families.

Being back at the mini-ranch on leave was heaven and all too short a break. For a brief moment my time was my own. No one was constantly shouting at me. I could get a full night's sleep. My dress, activity and entertainment were of my choosing. I wasn't living in the snow. I was surrounded by people who cared about me—who had no desire to be constantly inspecting my living quarters or judging me. I could sleep in past 5 a.m. I could take long showers in a bathroom

I didn't have to share with a dozen other guys. I could come and go as I pleased. I could eat what I wished. I could spend my days with a beloved and beautiful woman. It was heaven.

My eating habits had changed, though I didn't realize it until this visit home. All my life I had been a slow eater, generally the last one at the table to finish. It seems that a few weeks of drill sergeants yelling at me to hurry up and eat ("This ain't no damn dayroom!") had sped up my eating. MaryAnne was amazed at the way I wolfed down meals.

We didn't visit many people aside from my family and hers. It was clear that my entire family was happy to see me, and it was wonderful to have time to talk with Mom. My little sister, Mary, practically became glued to my lap. We saw a few close friends but MaryAnne and I mostly kept to ourselves, valuing every hour and enjoying each other's company. We went on drives, took walks, talked, went to movies (I recall *The Lion in Winter*, *Bullitt* and *The Thomas Crown Affair* especially) and listened to music: Chuck Berry, Elvis, the Beatles, Tommy Edwards, the Stones, the Beach Boys, Simon and Garfunkel, and more.

Before I knew it, my leave was over and we were at the airport. To say it was difficult to go off again doesn't tell the half of it. Saying goodbye to family before we left Napa was hard enough, but saying goodbye to MaryAnne at the airport was hell. I thought she was never going to let go of me, and it was just as hard for me to let go of her. It was heartbreaking when I had to turn around and walk away.

Upon my return to Fort Lewis, we were "volunteered" to give blood. Needles had always made me a bit woozy, and by this point I was angry at myself over this issue. I determined that I would continue to give blood until such time as I was able to do so without being lightheaded. I had no way of knowing that this lightheaded business was going to cease to be a problem after my second donation. Donating blood would end up as a regular practice for me, resulting in my contributing more than 11 gallons of blood over a number of years.

Toward the end of basic training, we were marched across the base to a large administrative building. There, each of us got to sit down and tell a young military clerk what job we might like to do in the army. When my turn at wishing came, I sat down in front of a young corporal, not much older or higher in rank than I was. I told him, "I want to do what you're doing." He looked at me quizzically, so I said, "I have a bachelor's degree in psychology. I've taken classes in personnel work and occupational choice." I may have had more training than he, but clearly he had the more powerful position, and I suppose he had the last laugh. He probably thought, Okay, you uppity jerk, I'll fix you right up. No desk job for you!

A couple weeks later, they posted the assignments for advanced training. I definitely did not get the desk job I had requested from the corporal. But I was relieved and grateful to learn that I had been assigned to the artillery. Most of those men with college experience or degrees were headed for the infantry, the part of the army that does the real fighting. The heavy artillery, while critical, is often based somewhat behind the lines and fires its cannons at a distance. It's still a dangerous business, of course, but generally not quite as risky as having to walk into the bush to engage the enemy.

Ron and Jarrold got artillery, too. I felt great about the fact that I would be going to Fort Sill, Oklahoma, with a couple of my best buddies, but I couldn't help feeling somewhat guilty that most of my guys were headed for much more dangerous assignments than I was. I feared for their safety. My sadness and regret regarding those men have never completely left me, even though I had no control over their assignments.

A few days later we were on the parade field, standing in formation in several inches of snow, about to graduate. Our commanding officer congratulated us for having gone through basic training in the worst winter that the state of Washington had seen in 50 years. My thought was, At least Vietnam will be warmer. We each received our private stripes that day.

10

WHAT A BLAST!

Some days later a few of us were transported from Fort Lewis to Fort Sill, home of the Army's artillery training center. Located in the southwest region of Oklahoma, Fort Sill is near the city of Lawton, which arose there because of the army base and not the other way around, or so I was told.

I was delighted to learn that my friend Pete had also been assigned to Fort Sill. The afternoon we arrived, we began the process of settling in, choosing a bunk, unpacking our duffel bags, and arranging gear and personal belongings in and around our footlockers in exactly the way the army expects to find them. The barracks accommodations were simple but adequate for the purpose, containing two floors of metal bunk beds and one wooden footlocker, or trunk, for each of the 40 to 50 men. One thing was equally simple but less adequate: the barracks themselves contained no latrine or showers. Those were located about 100 feet away and, of course, it was winter.

In the middle of our unpacking, the sergeant first class in charge of our platoon called for me to come and see him in the orderly room. Mac was a thin and crusty old-timer in his late 50s. Young GIs would refer to fellows like him as a "lifer" because he had spent most of his life in the army.

"I've been looking at your record. I see you've got a college degree and experience as a squad leader. I think you'd make a good platoon leader. What do you think?"

"I'm not sure. What would that entail?"

"You've watched other platoon leaders. You have a pretty good idea of what it requires. Rank does have its privileges."

As I stood there, I was thinking about KP and other lousy details that I wouldn't mind missing. Finally, I said, "Okay, Sarge. I'll give it a shot and do my best."

Mac told me I needed to choose an assistant platoon leader. I thought Pete would do a good job, so I asked him and he agreed. We decided I would live on the first floor and he on the second, so we could keep an eye on both floors. As far as I was concerned, things were starting to look a good deal rosier. But the truth is that I had no clue what I was getting into.

That evening, as Ron, Jarrold and I sat around polishing our boots, a good-sized man in civilian clothes entered the barracks with a very deliberate stride. He had two other fellows, also in civilian clothes, in tow. About 6 feet tall, in his 40s, with a hefty build, sharp facial features and a GI haircut, he was an imposing figure.

He walked boldly down the center of the barracks looking left and right. The expression on his face was angry. When he reached the far end of the barracks, he went upstairs. We had had a couple parents drop in to see their sons, so that's initially what I thought was happening. But this seemed different.

"Who was that guy?" Ron asked.

"I don't know," I said, "but I guess we'd better find out."

We went up the stairs to learn more. There we found the stranger addressing Pete in a very aggressive tone. Pete was standing at attention answering his questions. I stepped up and got the stranger's attention.

It turned out that he was the "First Sergeant" for our company: the highest-ranking non-commissioned officer. Mac was officially an E7 sergeant first class, a rank that is often in charge of a platoon. In contrast, a first sergeant generally oversees a company made up of several platoons. The first sergeant proceeded to chew my ass out for not confronting him when he first entered the building. He had a good point and I had no reasonable defense. This was the beginning of what was to be a very strained relationship, with him as the strainer and me as the "strainee." After this confrontation I had an uneasy feeling that being platoon leader wasn't going to be all that much fun.

It was still winter in Oklahoma. As it had in Washington, the weather made training a challenge. We were endlessly tired and often cold, but, much to our consternation, the weather conditions were decidedly variable. We got up in the morning and often went out to formation in the snow, dressed in various layers of army gear including an undershirt, long-sleeved fatigues, a heavy coat, and a poncho. But after breakfast, the platoon would often march to some other part of the base or out to the fields where the artillery was located, only to find that the snow had turned to rain. By lunch, the sun might be shining, leaving us hot and sweaty under all that gear and clothing; by afternoon the rain might return, and then later in the afternoon it would be snowing again. The old saying "If you don't like the weather, just wait a few minutes; it'll change" was never more true than in Oklahoma.

The United States Army has been firing cannons for over 200 years. They're pretty good at it, and training was well done. We trained on 105- and 155-millimeter howitzers. I learned a lot about both the smaller 105s, which fired a shell weighing 30 to 40 pounds, and the medium-sized 155s, which fired a shell weighing between 80 to 90 pounds. We naturally spent a good deal of time maintaining the cannons in top condition. In that sense we spent more time cleaning and polishing than we did actually firing the guns. (For more information on the technicalities of artillery, see the Appendix.)

Naturally, the men on base soon found ways to entertain themselves. Within the first week a number of them had figured out how to leave the base and find a bar. After drinking considerable quantities of beer, they would find their way home and go to bed. In the middle of the night Mother Nature would call, but the call was long distance: it was a 100-foot tiptoe through the snow to the latrine. Such a trip was bound to destroy any remnant of the alcoholic glow a soldier had gone so far out of his way to achieve.

Being creative thinkers, some men found relief by using the fire escapes rather than the latrines. Surely, this was not the first time some GI had used this strategy to relieve himself. Unfortunately, someone making rounds came across yellow holes in the snow and put two and two together. Accordingly, I was the unhappy recipient of another visit from the first sergeant, who ripped me 50 ways to Sunday for allowing such behavior. It mattered little that I was asleep while the infractions took place. Clearly, I wasn't in control of my men, a fact he planned to remedy by designating me as "piss guard" for the platoon.

It thus became my duty to stand outside in the snow at night with my rifle in hand and make sure that no one peed off the fire escape. I had that duty for about a week. Thankfully, the men took pity on me and stopped using the fire escapes as latrines before I had to shoot one of them. Just how they solved this problem I didn't ask. If the first sergeant's attempts at humiliation were intended to teach me something other than disdain for him, his efforts fell far short of the mark.

Training continued, including overnight campouts in the rain and snow. I was amazed at how few of my fellow GIs knew how or why to "trench" a tent when rain was on the horizon. Luckily, I understood both—I had never thought my Boy Scout training would be so handy. To trench a tent you simply take a small folding shovel or "trenching tool"—the army issued these—and dig a shallow trench a few inches deep around the perimeter of your tent. The trench draws water away from the tent and works best if you pitch the tent on a slight slant, so gravity also helps draw the water off. The two-man pup tents we used made for a tight squeeze, especially if you wanted to keep your pack as well as yourself out of the rain. I think the reason they called them pup tents is because they have enough room for one person and a pup rather than two full-sized humans. The hikes were not overly long but even when short, weren't much fun in foul weather. I must admit that I never got used to eating out of a mess kit in a downpour where I had no cover.

In theory, one of the benefits of being a platoon leader was exemption from kitchen patrol. "KP" consists of every dirty job that the cooks themselves don't want to do in the process of feeding large numbers of hungry men—in our case, roughly 200—from scrubbing floors to peeling potatoes. There's no way that I should have received KP duty, but I did. This was yet another gift from my nemesis, the first sergeant. I'm convinced he stayed up late thinking of ways to make my life miserable. There must have been something about me that truly bothered the man, but I was never able to put my finger on it. The antipathy was mutual. I can count on the fingers of one hand the number of people I have truly disliked in my life. My middle finger is reserved for this guy.

He did seem to think that Pete, my assistant platoon leader, was God's gift to the army. Pete would eventually be offered the opportunity to stay on as company clerk rather than go to Vietnam. He would accept, only to learn that the first sergeant liked him *too* much, and in a way that was thoroughly alien to Pete's own preferences. Happily for Pete, he was able to get himself transferred to another post, this time in South Korea.

One day, a portion of our training consisted of a presentation by two GIs from the United States Army Airborne School in Fort Benning, Georgia, commonly known today as the "Jump School." Their purpose was to recruit young men willing to jump out of an airplane into a war. As Jarrold, Ron and I sat listening to the presentation, a strange thought began to form among us—I don't recall whose idea it was specifically. We had been told that 98% of those graduating from artillery training would be going straight to Vietnam. We had also heard that some units were being withdrawn from that country, so it might just be a matter of time. Airborne training interested none of us, since jumping out of an airplane into a battle zone wasn't our idea of a good time. But we figured that if we could spend some time in it, perhaps we could delay the inevitable by another month or two. So all three of us signed up. Some might call such an action "plain stupid," but we saw it as less stupid than going straight to war.

When artillery training finally ended, Mac, our sergeant, informed us that Jarrold and I were going to airborne training. Ron, it turned out, had a bad back and didn't pass the necessary physical. He would be getting his orders for Vietnam, a reality that brought us all down. At that point there was nothing that could be done to change his fate. Jarrold and I felt horrible for him, and we knew we were living on borrowed time even though we were headed for Georgia rather than going directly to Vietnam. The war and what it represented became all the more real.

However, you could not keep Ron down for long. He was a force of nature. By the time we split up he had us convinced that he would be running his new outfit in no time at all. I told Ron, "Keep your head down and your powder dry."

He responded, "Keep your ass close to the ground and don't go jumping out of any damn airplanes."

That was definitely our goal. Jarrold and I grew cautiously optimistic that we could temporarily delay our tour of Southeast Asia by going airborne without really getting airborne, in the sense of jumping straight into battle. We had decided that having signed up for airborne training, we would drop out before it was necessary to put our new skills to use in an actual war zone. We knew we would catch hell for it, but so be it. With that scheme in mind, we prepared to leave Oklahoma for Georgia.

11

WHEN I SAY JUMP...

Our destination was Fort Benning, an army base just east of Columbus, Georgia, and the home of the army's parachute jump school. When we arrived, we were informed that they didn't yet have enough recruits to form a platoon and begin this newest round of training. They said it might be a week or two, so we settled in with the rest of the crowd, most of whom were young fellows 18 to 20 years old. Some were high school graduates, some had their GED (General Education Degree) and some had not graduated from any school in any way. For the most part they were physically fit and gung ho about being in the service.

Over the next week or two there was little to do other than sit around and talk, so that's what we did. We heard all the local rumors regarding what would happen if we bailed out of training—pun intended. Such weak-kneed cowards were sent to E Company, which was said to be home for the worst scum of the earth. A sergeant in the mess hall told us that E Company was so bad that the lieutenant had hung himself and the first sergeant had gone AWOL. Jarrold and I looked at each other with appropriate alarm. Company E must be filled with loons and criminals, we decided.

However, E Company was our "out" from jumping into war zones. So like it or not, our question became, "How do we join E Company?" Well, that brought a promising response. The sergeant told us that on the initial day of training, there would be a formation. At the formation the first sergeant would ask the group if there was anyone who did not want to participate in airborne training. If we were of that persuasion, we should immediately double-time to the front of the formation and present ourselves to the first sergeant.

But that chance was still in the future. In the meantime, we passed the time by talking or sitting in the dayroom. Ours contained its own black-and-white TV. As I've said, it was a time of considerable social upheaval among young people opposed to the draft and the war. Practically every newscast contained some information regarding who was protesting and where. The most significant protests seemed to center around Northern California's Bay Area. It was a common site to see a picket line of police with their usual sidearms (as well as nightsticks roughly 2 feet long) facing a crowd of irate but unarmed students. Violence was sporadic, with most of the conflicts remaining verbal. But when the confrontations did become violent, the students generally ended up getting the short end of the stick, as it were. Of course, African American citizens were also staging protests and marches, mainly in the Deep South, seeking equal treatment under the law and within society.

As Jarrold and I sat around for a couple weeks watching the war protests at UC Berkeley and my alma mater, San

Francisco State, on the old black-and-white TV, we naturally got into discussions regarding the war. Being draftees, our take on the military was often negative. From time to time some of the young men in the barracks would come and join us in conversation. We generally tried to discourage them from hanging out with us so that we could talk freely, without being accused of trying to incite discontent. We acknowledged that we were not terribly infatuated with the prospect of going airborne, but we had neither desire nor need to change their own opinions.

During any given discussion, they might hear one or both of us making statements such as, "There's a lot I don't understand regarding the history of this war, but I know the French were there before us for some years and they gave up and went home." Or, "It seems to me that you're biting off an awful lot to chew any time you step in the middle of a civil war." And, "Jumping out of an airplane into a war makes you a pretty easy target. I just don't like the odds. In the end, is the reward worth the risk?" Some would insist that they enjoyed the conversations and were determined to take part in our discussions despite these questioning perspectives.

The days passed, and suddenly it was the first day of training. On a beautiful Georgia day, we gathered in formation as directed. Just as we had been told he would, the first sergeant, a wiry fellow about 40 who was in charge of such assemblies, said something like "If anyone here does not want to take part in this training, he must report up here immediately." A blur flashed past me. Following it with my eyes, I saw that it was Jarrold double-timing to the front of the formation. I immediately took off after him. Though I was aware of other movement among the troops, I was aghast when I realized at last that there were maybe a dozen of us standing in front of the first sergeant. Most of them were young men who had taken part in our conversations over the past couple weeks. The first sergeant was beside himself. He didn't know whether to spit, swallow or chew. After he found his composure, he shouted, "All of you report immediately outside the company commander's office!"

We formed a single-file line outside the company commander's office and were told to enter one by one when our turn came around. The commander sat behind a government-issue wooden desk surrounded by government-issue standard office equipment, government-issue files, bookcases and a couple government-issue chairs and gave us what you might call a standard government-issue lecture.

I can only speak for my own meeting with him, but I learned later that they all went pretty much the same way. Standing at attention, I faced the company commander as he did his best to convince me that I should change my mind and go airborne. His rhetorical tools included flattery, cajoling, insults, and the calling of both my manhood and my loyalty to God and country into question.

"Troop, am I hearing correctly about you not wanting to go forward with your airborne training?"

"That is correct, sir."

"Then why did you sign up for training in the first place?"

"It seemed like a good idea at the time, sir."

"Nothing to be frightened of, Soldier. Thousands of men have done it."

"I have decided that I do not wish to parachute into a war, sir."

"I think you're acting like a little girl."

"I think I'm acting like an intelligent person, Sir."

And on the conversation went.

I didn't count how many caved and how many stood their ground. But one day later, the majority of us, who had remained steadfast, were marched across the base to the dreaded E Company. It was a lovely, sunny Sunday. As we approached, there was a good deal of activity, with men scurrying here and there in a park-like area from which came occasional shouts. As we came closer, we put two and two together and realized it was Easter. These dangerous and deviant felons were in the midst of an Easter egg hunt. It turned out that the person who found the golden egg would get a three-day pass.

Ironically, E Company turned out to be the best posting I had experienced thus far. Rather than gathering cowards, felons or deviants, it was simply a collection of men waiting for orders to come through. We were housed in standard barracks and treated no differently from other military personnel. The base itself was much like the other bases I had seen, simple basic buildings, kept clean and tidy by an unending supply of young soldiers.

Each day, I went out on 8-to-5 work details addressing what was needed on the base. During my time in E Company, I did such jobs as moving books for a library, painting whatever we were assigned to paint, and loading and unloading some bricks that were being moved for some reason… pretty routine stuff and much less uncomfortable than my training in Washington or Oklahoma. At the end of the workday, I would go to dinner. Then I was free to do as I wished the rest of the evening. One evening I went into town to see a movie. It was *Gone with the Wind*. I had never seen it, but it had to be a local favorite because it seemed to be playing permanently.

I was only in E Company about a week before my orders for Vietnam came through. Jarrold's came down a couple days later. We were going off for our "tour" in Vietnam. That's what the military called the time that we spent over there, a tour: an all-expense-paid chance to see a tiny little portion of the world. That was the bad news. The good news was that our orders included a 30-day leave prior to being shipped overseas. As unhappy as I was about my orders for Vietnam, I was very jazzed about the month's leave. I wasted no time catching a flight to the Bay Area and back to the arms of my sweet MaryAnne.

It seemed strange to me that the army would give me a month's vacation prior to sending me to Vietnam. It seemed like it was just giving reluctant soldiers a month's head start toward disappearing. But I guess the system worked well, or they wouldn't have continued the practice. It may have helped identify those likely to prove to be a problem later on. And having taken the oath, the penalties were definitely enough to deter one. As my good friend Cork figured out all too late, if you're going to say no, you should do so while you are still under civilian rules. If you balk once under military regulations, the military holds all the cards in a deck stacked against you.

At any rate, here I was at home spending precious time

with family and friends. Mom was clearly thrilled to see me. My stepdad Leigh played his usual subdued style but I could tell he was happy to see me too. The main difference was my two brothers, who had grown while I was gone. Together, they took me to the floor just to show me who was boss. Great fun.

Mostly, I cherished spending time with MaryAnne. When I was drafted, we had decided to continue paying our monthly rent at the mini-ranch, since it would cost almost that much to store our belongings elsewhere while I was gone. But MaryAnne had moved back home with her parents because the mini-ranch was on the edge of town and pretty isolated. Now, it didn't take us more than a couple hours to set up house again.

When MaryAnne had learned that I was coming home for 30 days, she knew that she didn't want to spend that time working. She had quit her job at the hospital before I arrived. We were free to spend time together at home, though we also took drives to "the city" as we referred to San Francisco, where there was always plenty to do. The toll to cross the Golden Gate Bridge was only 50 cents then, and often, just for the fun of it, we would pay for the car behind us. On occasion someone ahead of us paid for us. Perhaps it was a reflection of the "hippie" ethos that prevailed in the area at the time, but these acts of generosity and consideration were not at all uncommon. In the city we could spend time in Golden Gate Park, go to a museum, or wander around Union Square. Our favorite Italian restaurant was Bushati's on Lombard Street. We drove up the Napa Valley to enjoy some wine tasting, and we motored over to the coast and the

Pacific Ocean. I could not believe how sweet it was to be with my wife and to be free to do as I chose.

There was one other thing I wanted to do while I was home. That was to go see Elsie, the psychic in San Francisco. I had received good insights from a couple of earlier visits with her. She truly seemed to have a gift. I didn't claim then to know how it worked and I still don't know today. All I know is that she tapped into some energy, or base of information, that I could not access on my own behalf. Like my mother, Elsie read cards—but where Mom was pretty darn good, Elsie was a pro (and Mom would be the first one to agree with that).

Elsie was a grandmotherly type, gentle and soft-spoken. She lived in a second-story flat above a garage, a simple apartment on Lincoln Avenue close to the park. All these years later I clearly recall the main points of that reading. When asked about Vietnam, I recall her saying something like: "Yes, you will go to Vietnam, but don't worry, you will be fine. Angels will protect you. And you don't stay in Vietnam the whole time. About halfway through you leave Vietnam but you don't come back to the United States. You go to an island."

I told her I wanted to ask about a couple of friends. I didn't ask about Cork, because by then he was out of the army on a bad conduct discharge and safely back in Napa. My other buddy, Pete, had stayed at Fort Sill in Oklahoma as company clerk and would not be going to Vietnam either. Instead, I started with Ron, holding him in my mind as I cut the cards into three piles. Elsie looked at them and commented, "This fellow will be fine also. He always lands on his feet." Then I thought about Jarrold and cut the cards again. She looked at the cards once more. "Oh, my," she told me. "This fellow thinks he is already dead. But he will be fine also." Her insights about the characters of these men, whom she had never met, could not have been more on target. As I have said, Ron was the eternal optimist, always smiling and expecting the best, while Jarrold was a classic pessimist who expected the worst to happen in every situation. The good news about them buoyed me considerably. I could only hope Elsie was right.

Once Elsie explained that I would be leaving Vietnam and going to an island, MaryAnne reasoned that it would be somewhere with a U.S. government operation. She applied for a job at the Pittsburgh Naval Weapons Station in the Bay Area. She was hired there to do administrative work related to ship manifests. Her hope was to be transferred to wherever I was stationed some day, so we might be together. Sure, it was a long shot. But when you're dealing with a war, all your shots are long ones. Besides, we had good reason to trust Elsie's insights.

Speaking of long shot, some time toward the beginning of my 30-day leave MaryAnne and I found ourselves in the midst of a conversation on the topic of starting a family.

I said, "It's a big question. How do you feel about it?"

"I don't know. You're only here for a month. We could just continue on and if it happens, it happens. If it doesn't, it doesn't. Let fate take its course."

I responded, "That seems okay with me. If it happens, we'll live with it. And I really mean we will live with it…well, with him or her!"

Nothing lasts forever, no matter how wonderful it might be. My 30-day leave ended all too quickly. MaryAnne and my mother took me to airport for my flight to Vietnam. It was a tearful goodbye, one of the most painful experiences of my life. It's difficult to express the emotions you feel when you're not sure you'll ever see your loved one again. I could see MaryAnne's heart was breaking, and there was nothing I could do about it. My reassurances sounded hollow. No magic words could ease the pain of what was ahead. All we could do was hang on to Elsie's assurance that angels would protect me and all would be well.

One last kiss, and I finally had to turn and walk to the plane.

12

WELCOME TO THE WAR

At the airport, I bumped into Jarrold. We were both headed for Vietnam, but we would go in different planes and head in different directions once there. We had been through a lot together, and it was great to see him.

"Jarrold," I said. "Good to see you. How was your leave?"

"Too damn short! How was yours?"

"The same," I said. "But I saw a really good psychic, and she assured me that you would be fine over there."

He looked at me as if I had suffered a psychotic break. I hadn't expected anything else; I knew such thoughts would sound crazy to most people. I just smiled, said I looked forward to seeing him again, and told him I hoped to get together with him and Ron when we all returned.

My flight had a stopover in Honolulu, though we were not let off the plane. It was odd looking out the window at a place I had first visited at age 19 with friends and returned to for our honeymoon three years later. What great memories! I wondered what kind of memories I would have of Vietnam, assuming I got back okay.

Our next stop would be Guam, after which we would finally reach Vietnam. It was a long flight, with all too much time to think. As I've said earlier, I had seen copious footage of the war on the news. The clashes in the jungles looked dangerous, miserable and very damn scary. It's one thing to imagine someone shooting at you; it was even worse to think about walking into some of the booby-traps the enemy had devised. I really had no idea what I was getting into, I just assumed it would not be good. Most of us on the plane were pretty quiet except for a couple of nervous chatterers. Someone finally told them to pipe down. It wasn't a time for conversation; everyone seemed lost in his own thoughts.

I was sitting in an aisle seat, so I didn't have a great view out the window when Vietnam came into sight. From what I could see there were flat areas and rolling hills, with a mixture of green vegetation and what must have been rice paddies all spotted with large patches of bare ground. I found out later that those brown areas were inhabited by the military, which had no inclination to keep things green and pretty.

But the sight of Vietnam caused something in me to shift. Some primal, survival-driven part of my brain took over any and all other thoughts, opinions or beliefs. Suddenly, it was very clear that I needed to do anything I could to stay alive and return home. My brain was telling me, "Get real. This is serious." My fundamental resistance to this war didn't change, but I knew the time for games, doubts and delaying strategies was over.

We landed in the Bien Hoa military base and were directed to a C-47 Skytrain. This cargo plane would take us to Da Nang and then to Quang Tri, located about 115 miles from

Da Nang at the northern end of South Vietnam in Quang Tri Province.

It was a decidedly uncomfortable flight, limited as we were to bench seats in a windowless transport plane mainly intended for hauling freight.

Once we landed, we were taken to a part of the base meant for people in transit. From there, I was one of four people in our group headed for Fire Support Base Charlie 2. Other than that, I knew nothing. I had learned that the military generally had little concern for giving you details or filling in background, probably because they didn't give you much choice, either. As a private I was generally told only what I absolutely needed to know. In a situation such as this it left a lot to the imagination.

If you're not familiar with phonetic code and you're wondering who "Charlie" is, let me clarify. The U.S. military, among other institutions and organizations, uses the International Radiotelephony Spelling Alphabet (also called the ICAO phonetic alphabet or NATO alphabet), which was developed in the 1950s to clarify communications, especially over weak or muddled radio frequencies. Using "Beta" instead of "B," "Charlie" instead of "C," and "Delta" instead of "D" among other replacements differentiates among letters with similar sounds, allows letter/number combinations to be voiced clearly, and avoids dangerous confusion in critical instructions. Hence, Fire Support Base C-2 was known as "Charlie 2." While on the subject of nomenclature, I should add that the "fire" in "fire support base" refers not to flames or blazes but to gunfire. In other words, Charlie 2 was military outpost heavily fortified with various forms of artillery intended to support troops out in the bush.

Just to make sure we would not get bored while we waited to move on to Charlie 2, we were led to a pile of sand and a stack of sandbags and told to fill them up. It must have been about 110° to 115° that afternoon. One by one we each succumbed to the heat and became nauseated. I never knew whether the work was actually necessary or whether this was how they welcomed all the "new boots." Suddenly the cold and changeable weather of my earlier army bases didn't seem so bad.

We were housed that evening in a tent large enough to walk around in, with a wooden floor and sleeping cots. That first night "in country" (a military term referring to a foreign country rather than a rural place), I tried to sleep without success. In the distance, I could hear small-arms fire along with an occasional explosion. When I stood up and looked out of the tent, I could see a tower on fire maybe 150 yards away. The fact that I was in a war zone suddenly became very real.

The next morning, the four of us were loaded into the back of a military pickup truck for the ride from Dong Ha to our new home. The road between Quang Tri and Charlie 2 was densely studded with landmines and snipers, sure bets to get the adrenaline flowing. The countryside was dotted with rice paddies and other vegetation, a deceptively serene and peaceful landscape. That day we reached our destination without incident, but my travels in the area would not always be so calm.

Charlie 2 was about 5 miles from the demilitarized zone, or DMZ, between North and South Vietnam. If you were to wander a few minutes in the wrong direction, you could find

The view from Charlie 2, 1969

Fire Support Base Charlie 2, 1969

yourself in deep trouble, though I don't think any of us had the energy or inclination to roam around. Located at the top of a hill—an advantage in military terms, I'm told—the base was a few acres of barren dirt amid a sea of dense vegetation only 3 or 4 feet high. Thanks to its lack of vegetation, on first glance it had the appearance of a strange, mechanized anthill. In addition to its guns, Charlie 2 had a headquarters hut, mess hall, latrines, showers, and barracks, which were called "hooches." That slang (and in some cases, derogatory) term is generally used to refer to thatched Asian huts, but at Charlie 2 we used the word for the barracks that were our living quarters.

The base was surrounded with concertina wire in a defensive effort to slow down the advance of any North Vietnamese Army soldiers or Vietcong fighters that might come our way. The former were organized military troops and the latter were unofficial guerilla combatants, often local residents, but both were fighting against the U.S. (Our allies were the ARVN, the Army of the Republic of Vietnam.) On occasion, I would hear that the enemy had attacked some portion of the perimeter, but they never breached our position while I was there.

The climate of the base was as noticeable as its structures and "attractions." The rainy season in Vietnam, which runs roughly from late June to October, features an average of about 14 inches a month of rainfall in the tropical pattern, with heavy rain falling daily in short bursts rather than softer or more gradual rainfall. We arrived in April, so the rainy season would not yet be in full force for the first couple months. But the heat was nasty. With the pervasive humidity, the heat became among the most noticeable features of my new life.

With military promptness, I was introduced to my sergeant, Jason. (I'm sorry to say that I don't recall his last name or that of some of the other men I served with.) He was a large and imposing African American usually seen smoking a cigar. He looked to be in his mid-30s, about 6'5" tall and 275 pounds. He had a nonchalant air about him, but I sensed very clearly that he was not someone you would ever want to cross. He took me to the "hooch" where I would be living. All living quarters at Charlie 2 were partially dug into the ground, with sturdy 12" x 12" beams making up the frames and wooden floors. Mounds of sandbags and other reinforcements were piled on the top of each "hooch." There were plenty of nooks and crannies to create homes for the rats. The entrances at both ends of each hooch were curving passages so an enemy could not fire directly into the living quarters.

I would soon learn one of the most dramatic aspects of the hooches at Charlie 2. For reasons totally beyond my understanding, someone had placed Gun 3, nicknamed "Irene," such that it fired generally and sometimes even directly over the my hooch from only about 20 yards away. When Gun 3 had a fire mission during the day, the blasts that shook the hooch and rattled your fillings could be unsettling, especially to us new men. At night, the noise and reverberations were downright maddening. The muzzle blasts would literally lift us off our bunks an inch or so; the ever-present dirt and sand would fall on us from above and the noise of the blasts was nearly deafening.

Jason introduced me to the half of the crew that wasn't

Gun 4 hooch, "Home Sweet Home"

currently serving its shift at the gun. As he introduced me to each one individually, I couldn't help but notice that most of the crew was black. I shook hands with each one in turn and received a generally cool reception, which I assumed was standard, until I got to TP (I never heard him referred to in any other way). This short but sturdy African American fellow turned from his footlocker to face me, ignoring my outstretched hand, and said words to the effect of, "Look, you sorry son-of-a-bitch, don't ever speak to me! You have nothing to say to me and I have nothing to say to you. So keep your goddamn thoughts to yourself. I could care less what you think about anything. Stay out of my face and stay out of my life, you sorry bastard!" I may have gotten some of the specifics of this speech wrong, but what I'm certain about is that I've seriously tidied up its language.

I stood there in shock. Unsure how to reply, I decided finally that no reply was necessary, much less desired. I was frightened at the level of his anger and his apparent hatred, both delivered at short range and face-to-face. It was impossible to forget that everyone present had access to deadly weapons and the training to use them, though I didn't expect TP or anyone else go that far. But that knowledge certainly added to the level of tension present in the battery. I had had "my hair blown back" a time or two at San Francisco State by angry black males but never to this degree.

Later, one of the Caucasian soldiers explained that TP held the leadership position within the unofficial group of African American enlisted men within the battery. I have no proof of that, but his peers did seem to treat him with a certain amount of deference. He clearly had the attributes of a leader.

I have since thought more deeply about TP's background, as well as the realities of that era, in trying to understand him better. As I've said before, this was a time when relations between blacks and whites were strained. TP was small in stature and came from the streets of Chicago. Being introduced to me in front of his black "brothers" may have made him feel it necessary to demonstrate strength or dominance, and it's easy for me to believe that he felt the deck was stacked against him. I could hardly blame African Americans for being angry when being drafted to fight the war for a country that treated them like second-class citizens. I'm sure he had plenty of reasons to be angry.

Today, I'm also more aware of the way differences in class and affluence affect the military. As a result of poverty and lack of other choices, far more young people of color served in the military of the time than whites, a disproportion that has continued to some degree to this day. I might have been drafted, but I'd had the luxury of being able to defer my military service by pursuing higher education, and I could have fled to Canada had I chosen to do so. For many minorities, those options were largely unavailable.

Of course, none of this occurred to me at the moment. Shocked by his verbal assault, I just stood in silence. Now finished with me, TP returned his attention to his footlocker. The sergeant, who had been present throughout this interaction, acted as though nothing had happened. As he moved on to show me more of the base, I asked the sergeant if TP gave all new guys this type of welcome. The sergeant responded neutrally, "He may be having a bad day."

We walked up to where our gun, a large cannon designated "Gun 4," was located and I was introduced to the weaponry amid which I would be serving. I'll talk about that gun and my work on and around it later.

The gun crew generally consisted of 12 to 14 men and was split into two groups, with each group taking a 12-hour shift. I had already been introduced to half the crew back in the hooch. Now I was introduced to the crew that was "on the gun" for their 12-hour shift. I would be part of this crew, which I noted was all white. Not a big deal, but I might have wished for a bit more diversity within the crews.

The fact that my crew was on during the day meant that I would begin by sleeping in the hooch at night. In a week, when the shift would change, my crew would sleep on the gun. Not literally on the gun, though that was the term we used, but with it.

Once I'd met the guys on the gun, the sergeant told me to go back to the hooch and unpack my gear. After that I could go to lunch. I guess unpacking my possessions took a little longer than I had anticipated. I eventually got to the mess hall, a good-sized flat top wooden building with layers of sandbags on top. Large enough to hold 60 or 70 people, it was already full when I arrived there. I grabbed a tray and got in the chow line. I would discover that the food was pretty decent, usually including some type of meat, a starch (usually potatoes), vegetables of one sort or another and generally a dessert.

Once I had my lunch in hand, I turned and looked for a place to sit. Most of the tables were full except for a couple of them pushed end to end. One of those tables was empty and the other half filled, entirely by non-whites. All of the soldiers I could see who were members of minority groups were gathered there.

There were a few spots that I could have chosen to squeeze into with white folks, but that wasn't my inclination. I was still stinging from the special welcome TP had given me in the hooch and I wanted to make a sort of statement: in essence, "If this is a game, I don't want to be on either side." I looked at the situation and thought, "Hey, I'm new. It's my first day. I can act dumb and get away with this at least once." So I walked to the middle of the empty table, sat down, and began to eat.

When I looked up, I saw that most of the guys in the mess hall were looking at me with what I took for surprised curiosity. Those in the minority contingent at the other end of the table were giving me their undivided attention. I'm sure now that my "statement" was interpreted in a variety of ways, few of which I actually intended. But there was no repercussion that I was aware of except for cold stares, including one from TP. Sadly, I received no future invitations to dine at the minority table—I suppose they must have misplaced my phone number.

Racial or ethnic tensions weren't the only ways in which the mess hall kept us on our toes. On occasion the Vietcong would rudely interrupt our breakfast, lunch or dinner with a few rockets. Mess was just about the only time that everyone on base gathered in one place, so had they hit the mess hall directly, the impact on Charlie 2 would have been huge. But the good news was the VC had no accurate method of aiming their rockets. Still, it did tend to disrupt our meal when we had to get up and run for cover. Fortunately, this was not a frequent occurrence, happening maybe every couple of weeks or so. Whoever first heard a rocket would holler "Incoming!" and we would all make a mad dash to take cover.

I quickly learned that the gun crew to which I had been assigned contained some interesting characters. One of my buddies on the gun was Jim, affectionately referred to as the Tennessee Ridge Runner. He was a "good ol' boy" and we had some fun singing country songs. I recall working with him on one of his first fire missions, when the demand to fire became intense. We were running our asses off trying to keep up. Such moments, when you're both busting your butts with maximum physical output, let you see what someone is made of. After a few minutes of this, Jim looked at me as we picked up another 200-pound shell and said, "They really want to play kick-ass, don't they?" with a big

Music session in Vietnam, 1969: "Anybody know this one?"

smile on his face. That told me all I needed to know.

Another fellow I got to know pretty well there on Gun 4 was Ed, who I often called Fast Eddie. There was something mysterious about Ed. He claimed to have been born with a veil over his face. He might have meant that he had been born covered by a caul, or partial amniotic sac, which was once held to be lucky. Whatever he meant, it added to his mystery. I vividly recall the times I saw Ed sit with someone holding a deck of cards. Ed would try to read the other person's mind to guess what card the fellow was holding. He was surprisingly accurate, apparently beyond mere chance. He had a dry sense of humor and I liked him a lot.

Then there was Tom Villano. Tom was a member of the crew on Gun 3, which was right next to my hooch. As I walked past Gun 3 on my first day, he took the opportunity to make a smart-ass remark. I can't recall the remark itself, just that it was witty and stinging in a playful sort of way. It was an A-1 conversation starter.

Perhaps a few times in your life you're lucky enough to meet someone with whom you click immediately, someone you know from the start that you can trust. Such was the case with Tom. He was a high-quality human being and became my best friend in Vietnam, whether he knew it or not. Soldiers don't generally talk about such things openly and I was no exception. But we formed what would be a long friendship.

Tom was a surfer from Torrance, California, and a talented guitar player. He owned a beautiful, biting sense of humor that grabbed me from the start. Our friendship grew quickly. Having been on base for several months when I arrived, he had information and know-how that I sorely needed and that he was happy to share. Mostly he helped me understand how to get along in this new reality known as war.

Tom introduced me to another young fellow named Steve Bogacki. Steve explained that he had been hanging out on the streets of Chicago and didn't know what else to do with himself, so he joined the army. Another music lover, he also played guitar. Between them, Tom and Steve could play pretty much anything we requested, something for which the rest of us were very grateful.

13

GUNS BUT NO ROSES

During my first two nights at Charlie 2, I didn't get much sleep. "Irene," or Gun 3, had fire missions both nights and as I've said, I was painfully aware of them. My third night in country I was fortunate: I was able to sleep through the night for the very first time on the base.

The next morning, I got up and went down to breakfast in the mess hall. Choosing some eggs, bacon, potatoes and a cup of coffee, I sat down with the crew that had been on Gun 3 the night before. When I expressed my gratitude for the fact that we'd had no fire missions that night, Tom corrected me immediately. It seems they had fired several times, but I had failed to notice. Within only three nights, my brain had learned not to wake me up for something as inconsequential as a cannon blast. On the other hand, someone walking into the hooch in the middle of the night would wake me immediately. The fact is, the brain doesn't sleep. It's always on the job at some level, but it's also very skilled at adjusting itself to its environment. After that third night I had no more problems sleeping through cannon blasts.

The M-110 heavy howitzer, 1969

There were four 8-inch guns in our battery, although there were other groups of cannons of varying sizes elsewhere on the base. By the time I had arrived at Charlie 2, it was clear to me that my training on 105- and 155-mm howitzers would be of limited value. Both types of gun are considerably smaller than the cannon I would now be operating, the 8-inch self-propelled heavy howitzer M-110s. (For more on this gun, see the Appendix.) Essentially a huge cannon with tracks much like those of a tank, this gun fires a 204-pound projectile that is about 8 inches in diameter and about 3 feet in length. Hence the term "8-inch" howitzer. This was the largest cannon the army would use in Vietnam.

It generally takes a crew of six to operate this weapon. As I mentioned earlier, the crew of 12 to 14 men functioned as two groups, each taking a 12-hour shift. As in most situations, new guys start at the bottom. I began my tour in the "projo," or projectile pit, working in tandem with another soldier to wrestle 204-pound shells to the back of the gun. The ground between the projo pit and the back of the gun was a rutted, bumpy mixture of mud and gravel constantly churned up by rainfall and the motion of men and machines. We often found ourselves up to our shins in mud. Between the uneven surface and the weight of the projectiles (along with their 30-pound carrying racks) it was tough going even during the day, much less at night. I've seen more than one guy lose a boot trying to make it to the back of the gun with the needed projo.

We could fire a couple of times per minute during the most intense engagements. Every one of the crewmembers would be moving, trying to complete all of the necessary tasks quickly but with the required precision. To say the least, such "fire missions" kept us very busy. How busy? As my dad, Red, used to say, "Busier than a cat covering up crap on a marble-top desk with a sore paw and going to town for dirt."

If one of the rockets that the Vietcong liked firing ever hit a projo or powder pit directly, it would be very bad news to everything and everyone nearby. That possibility was just another thing I couldn't dwell on, so I would try to put it out of my mind as best I could while in the thick of a fire mission. I've always thought that beyond their physical strength, one reason that the army likes to use soldiers between the ages of 18 and 26 in battle is because such youths think they're immortal, and tend to believe against all odds that "it will never happen to them." I suppose I had some of that attitude myself.

When I was on the gun, I had to be ready for a fire mission

at any time. I discovered that the artillery is rather like a baseball game. You can stand around for quite a while with nothing happening. Then all of a sudden all hell breaks loose and your focus is intensely channeled into the task at hand. This was especially true for the guys manning the projo pit, as well as the lone chap in the powder pit—those were the most physically taxing duties. The other three men operating the gun had places up on the gun itself, which wasn't quite as strenuous.

The nature of our fire missions varied in their intensity and duration; the time between shells could vary from one minute to an hour. There was no way to predict how our time on the gun would go, as it depended on what was happening out in the bush.

*Fire mission underway, **1969***

One day the sergeant asked me if I had ever owned a vehicle that I had to care for and maintain. I told him that I had owned seven vehicles in all from the time I was 15 on. He then told me that he was making me the driver of Gun 4 and it would be my responsibility to take care of it. What could I say?

I liked vehicles of all types, though I had certainly never had the opportunity to drive anything with tracks. And in truth, that opportunity wouldn't come just now, either. The gun never actually went anywhere, making the title of driver a bit misleading, if not downright excessive. My new role just meant that I was the person assigned to take care of minor maintenance on the gun, checking the fluid levels and such. However, if there came a time that the battery moved, I stood a good chance of driving Gun 4. I still have my military driver's license that shows that I am qualified not only to drive several types of trucks but also a self-propelled 8-inch howitzer.

As time went on, the routines of Charlie 2 became second nature to me. One involved water buffalos, though not the kind you may be picturing. The base had no natural source of water, so it had to be trucked in. The "water buffalo," as we called it, was a large water tank on wheels that could be towed by a small truck and that held several hundred gallons of water. On the back end was a faucet that could be worked by hand. If you carelessly opened the faucet fully, you would get a whole lot more water than you wanted.

Thanks to the water buffalo, our water supply wasn't a problem, by and large, unless some guy up ahead took too long a shower. One day I saw an ARVN soldier walk up to a water buffalo to get a drink. He bent over, cupped his hands, spilled a little water into his hands, took a drink from his cupped palms, washed his face and his hands with the remaining water, and walked away. He used no more than a cup of water in total. Not far behind him was an American soldier who went to the same faucet, turned it on full blast, cupped his hands and took a drink. By the time he turned it off he had dumped a couple gallons of water on the ground. I was immediately embarrassed, realizing that if it were me getting that drink, I would have done much the same as the American soldier. We're so used to abundance that we think little of wasting that which would be precious to others.

And speaking of waste, Charlie 2 produced a good deal of garbage that had to be disposed of. The men on garbage detail would get on the garbage truck to go to the dump. We were sure to take our M-16s with us, since we were leaving the post. Another reason for the rifles: one man's garbage is another man's survival, and the poor Vietnamese peasants from around the area would usually be waiting at the dump for the arrival of our castoffs. Troops on the garbage truck would sometimes have to fire their weapons in the air trying to keep Vietnamese children as young as seven from climbing onto the truck while it was still moving. They would grab what we considered waste foodstuffs and throw them down to their families. It was a desperate free-for-all. Remembering that scene still brings me sadness all these years later. It's so easy to be unappreciative of our abundance. I was beginning to realize that reluctant as I had been to come to Vietnam to fight and risk my life, like my fellow American soldiers I was still a privileged person in many ways.

My warm beer at day's end, 1969

"Love what you've done with the place."

As noted earlier, the very hot, humid climate was really challenging. Work assignments each day were generally tackled right after breakfast in order to get tasks accomplished before the hottest part of the day. During the afternoon you could find me either on the gun or hanging out in the vicinity of the hooch.

Despite its limitations, the hooch felt like home (of a sort, at least) by this point. Under my bunk, my footlocker held personal items. Attached to the wall above my bunk was a small shelf that held family photos, soft drinks, a drinking cup and, often, a jar of Tang. (For those unfamiliar with Tang, it's a powder that makes an orange-flavored beverage when added to water…not exactly an organic delight, but much appreciated in Vietnam.) We shared the hooch with the ever-present rats, mostly heard rather than seen. Our not-so-little nocturnal friends only showed up after lights out. I can still remember the first time I felt one crawling across my chest in the dark. Coached by the men who had been at Charlie 2 longer, I quickly learned not to react too violently to avoid being bitten. A rat bite could mean a trip to the rear base for a series of rabies shots in the stomach.

Once in a while, we were inspired to put crumpled paper on the floor of the hooch with some kind of food on it. We would get out our bayonets and turn off the light. When we heard the paper really start rustling, someone would flip on the light and everyone would throw their bayonet at the rats that had come out to feed. They were pretty quick and I don't think we ever got one.

Life in the hooch was lived at close quarters. Several guys had their own cassette stereos set up, and, naturally, their choices in music diverged. Black soldiers were often into Motown: this was the heyday of the Supremes, Marvin Gaye, the Four Tops and soul music generally. The Southern white boys were most likely into Country and Western, then dominated by musicians like Merle Haggard, Glen Campbell, Johnny Cash, and Tammy Wynette. And then there were the rock 'n rollers, who liked the Beatles, the Rolling Stones, Cream, the Doors, Dusty Springfield and Simon and Garfunkel.

Other hooches may have played other music, but that was what ours listened to. And when we sat around with guitars and sang along, the repertoire often included a heavy dose of folk and protest songs by Bob Dylan, Pete Seeger, Joan Baez, Arlo Guthrie, and Peter, Paul and Mary.

I personally enjoyed all of these different types of music, but, sadly, they didn't mix well. One guy would have his music on and someone else would come in and turn on *his* music. Then the first guy would turn up the volume a bit and the second guy would do the same, and pretty soon we had the battle of the bands in full blast. It was just another cause of friction for guys living in cramped conditions in a stressful environment. Generally, guys were pretty good at keeping their cool. But living together in tight quarters during a war isn't easy.

In addition to the inevitable fire missions, the average day also included the challenge of staying hydrated in heat that would frequently be 115 to 120 degrees; work details as assigned; and, of course, the requisite three trips to the mess hall for meals. Somewhere in the course of each day I would do the same things GIs have done forever—write letters home—since, unlike some, I was lucky to have someone that I wanted to write to. When not on the gun, I might be listening to music, playing some card game, re-reading a book (I had quickly finished the final book in the Lord of the Rings trilogy) or old letters from home, or sleeping. I could take a shower if there was water, or I could sit and shoot the breeze with some buddies. In general, when you were on duty, a good tactic was to stay out of sight or at least look busy.

Guys like me were lucky enough to get care packages from home. Those were a real treat; they were always a great surprise and the contents beat the hell out of a hard biscuit from a C-ration can. (You had to be really hungry to break one of those open.) But not all breaks to the routine were good. On occasion there were distractions such as helicopters. They only seemed to come around for two reasons. Either someone was hurt and this was a Medevac, or it was a helicopter gunship. The latter were usually known as "Puff" because of the way their machine guns breathed fire.

Neither one was good news; one meant that someone was hurt, while the other meant that the enemy was nearby. Sometimes at night I would see Puff firing its machine guns with tracer rounds; it made for an eerie light show. I tried not to think about what was happening at the other end of that line of bullets, just as I tried to avoid thinking about where our cannon shells were falling as we executed a fire mission. But avoiding such thoughts was difficult to do.

Now and then I would be on guard duty, naturally a tense exercise in paranoia. We got to use fascinating night-vision equipment, but somehow that still didn't make it all that much fun. It was an intense job that had me constantly wondering if I had really seen some kind of movement or if it was just my imagination. It was always a relief to see the sun come up.

14

WHO KNOWS WHAT'S IN THE CARDS?

As I've said, I was one of those lucky guys with a wife anxious to send me letters several times a week. Those missives were often filled with various news items regarding the family. Since MaryAnne had seven brothers and sisters, there was never a shortage of news. I loved getting those letters.

After I'd been in country just a few weeks, a letter that changed my world arrived. MaryAnne broke the news to me that she was pregnant! I was in the hooch when I read the letter, and I started yelling out loud at the news. My feelings ran the gamut from shock to disbelief to excitement to concern to confusion to acceptance to joy and back through all those feelings again. In the end I was ecstatic. Naturally, the guys in the hooch gave me a bad time, suggesting some other rooster had gotten in the henhouse in my absence. Then came the many congratulations. We immediately broke out a few of the beers we had stashed away from our daily allotment and celebrated the wonderful news.

From then on, MaryAnne's letters added updates on her pregnancy to other family news. These letters were bittersweet. I looked forward to getting them and was delighted when they came, but there was always of an element of sadness in reading them. They made me miss her even more.

Thanks to MaryAnne's books, which described the development of a child from conception to birth, each letter made the fact of our baby's existence feel more real to me. For instance, one letter told me, "the child now has fingernails." Today, couples can see their growing baby in real time on a sonogram. Thinking about things like the baby's fingernails wasn't anywhere near that dramatic, but it too takes one's sense of "baby" from a vague concept closer to a glimpse of an actual human being.

I would frequently think about the evolving nature of our family. Big changes were coming, and my life would never be the same. I was to be a father! Would it be a boy or girl? Either way I was taking on a brand-new level of responsibility. The thought was rather daunting, but I was sure that together, MaryAnne and I would make a wonderful home for whoever was on the way. And although we picked out a name for each possible gender, we tended to refer to the child as Matthew rather than Melinda. I'm not sure why—maybe just a hunch. Later, MaryAnne proudly sent me a black-and-white photo of herself in the backyard, demonstrating that she could no longer button her jeans.

My mother, always a big letter writer, also kept me up-to-date on developments on the home front. Her letters—whose stationery changed from time to time—tended to be a blend of family news, her thoughts regarding spiritual matters, and her response to any questions or concerns I'd shared in my own recent letters. Her early letters to me in Vietnam were written in pencil in a lovely cursive script. Eventually she rented a typewriter, on which she became quite proficient. Her letters were not as frequent as MaryAnne's because she tended to write over a period of days before mailing a major missive, adding typed or handwritten thoughts as she had them. On occasion I was lucky enough to receive one with doodles in the margin. Mom was an ardent doodler, and her scribbles were always fun to look at, sometimes geometric and sometimes cartoonish but always interesting. The artist in her just couldn't be still. She most often wrote in the dead of night when the rest of the family was fast asleep, and the letters would often go on page after page. What a delight!

As I read her letters over time, I sensed that her view of the war was changing. Then one day I got a letter from her in which she said, "If anything happens to you over there, Don, I will never be able to look at that flag again." I knew she had tears in her eyes when she wrote those words. She loved that flag almost as much as she loved me. As I read the words I had a real sense of sadness, not for myself but for the heartache and fear she was living with every day. Her words brought home the fact that in some sense, soldiers' families went to war right along with them.

Her words were also a powerful measure of how much the Vietnam War had shaken America. The trust and pride in fighting a necessary and just war that had sustained the U.S. during World War II were breaking down. We couldn't know it yet, but Vietnam would permanently change the way Americans regarded wars and the government. The war touched them with doubt and suspicion that was new—and for staunch patriots like my mother, deeply disheartening.

While I was in the army, MaryAnne made it a point to go over once a week and visit my mother and their relationship strengthened and deepened. Mom had read MaryAnne's cards on numerous occasions before I was drafted; around the time MaryAnne became pregnant, my mother started reading cards for her every week. Each week, while having her cards read, MaryAnne would make a wish that she and I would be together for the birth of the baby. Each week the answer in the cards came back, "Yes." When MaryAnne passed this information on to me in her letters, my reactions were mixed. I believed that it was possible, but I was puzzled about how it could possibly come about.

When I was writing home, I had to be careful about what I said. My family was stressed out enough just having me in Vietnam, and of course I wanted to spare MaryAnne all possible worry during her pregnancy. I tended to leave out news that was negative and worrisome, such as incoming rockets or other dangerous events. For instance, I deliberately failed to mention being the crew's machine gunner.

That assignment began when my sergeant delivered a pronouncement. He (or somebody above him) had decided that the top of the projo pit really needed a machine-gun nest. First he showed us a picture of what he had in mind. Then he ordered some of the guys, including me, to build it. We had enough lumber already at hand. It took us a few days but we finished it. Once we were finished, the sarge showed up with a 50-caliber machine gun—a gun that was effective against infantry and lightly armored vehicles—and announced that I would be the 50- caliber guy. The machine gun was my responsibility to take care of and fire.

If you're a young man living long enough among men who are young, gung ho and macho, you probably can't help but have some of the machismo rub off on you, even though at some level you know that it's kind of stupid. I was an old man of 24, married and with a child on the way. Yet I couldn't help taking some pleasure at being the machine-gun guy. The downside, however, was that I was little more than a sitting duck for any invading force. My elevated position also served as an ideal target for incoming explosives; if one had hit the projo pit beneath me, no one would ever find my many pieces. I thank my lucky stars that I never had to man that machine gun in an actual attack. When we later got a new commanding officer he asked, "Who is the idiot that thought that was a good idea?" He had us tear that machine-gun nest down.

When entertaining other brass one day, a commanding officer decided that it would be fun to show off the firepower of our 8-inch howitzer. He commanded one of the guns to fire at a nearby hill. Since the shrapnel can carry as far as the projectile itself (and kill you just as efficiently), the troops who had fired the gun, as well as anyone else in the general vicinity, went frantically diving for cover as shrapnel came flying back in their direction. One good-sized piece actually lodged itself in the side of our powder pit. Fortunately, there were no injuries, except perhaps the tarnished pride of a certain officer. Dangerous moments can happen even when the enemy isn't involved.

As my time at Charlie 2 lengthened, my perceptions of the base were becoming clearer. From what I could see, the United States Army in Vietnam was a microcosm of what was going on back home, with many of the same heated tensions, particularly racial ones. What I had seen my first day in the mess hall was probably typical of what was happening in many places across the U.S. military.

I discovered that prior to my arrival some of the men on my gun had been transferred to other guns to create a more even distribution of racial diversity. I never did find out just how such moves worked out for the army. What I witnessed myself didn't suggest that they would accomplish much beyond, perhaps, creating a perception of integration. In the battery the tension between young white Southern boys and young black guys from around the country was palpable, and I noticed there was very little conversation between black and white enlisted men aside from army business.

One day I saw a young black soldier, newly arrived, whose camouflage helmet cover read, "We have to live together." When I saw him the following day those words were all crossed out. Something had changed overnight. Who or what caused this change I can only guess.

But the incident with TP had lit some kind of fire in me. Whether he actually saw me, a white man, as his enemy or had more complex, subtle feelings, I had no way of understanding—I just wasn't sure. But some part of me just couldn't let this "cold war" between us go unchallenged. If nothing else, I wanted him to know that I had no enmity towards him.

As I wrote to MaryAnne and my mother at the time, I began smiling when I saw him on a daily basis. I said, "Hi, how's it going?" when we passed each other. He responded with what I interpreted as disdain if he responded at all. Mostly he seemed to try to ignore me. We were on different gun crews, so we had little contact except in passing. In her letters my mother encouraged me not to give up or become discouraged. I figured I was driving him a little buggy as he wondered about this weird white guy who wanted to be his friend. I have to admit, I found that moderately amusing. But it was his friendship I was after, so I persisted.

One evening some of the guys on the crew were sitting around shooting the breeze in the hooch. As was often the case, the conversation came around to the war and how it was going. Various opinions and rumors were voiced. Some of the men had the notion that we were clearly winning the war and it might be over soon. Others felt the war would go on for a very long time. Thinking back to what Elsie had told me, I piped up, "I think it's possible that we might be pulled out. I heard that some troops have been withdrawn to Guam temporarily. There's a chance that we might be out of here in a few months."

Few in the group beyond me thought there was any chance of this. It was just pie in the sky. To this I replied, "Okay. Think what you want, but I think I'll be out of here before Christmas."

Their responses were along the lines of, "Oh sure, fat chance."

15

STAYING SANE IN A CRAZY PLACE

Given the opportunity, GIs will always find ways to blow off a little steam. There's nothing like a little sing-along to gladden the heart. A little smoking, a little joking and the world looks better.

Each soldier had a choice of two beers or two sodas at the end of the day. Some guys drank both right away and some saved one or both for later. Unfortunately, they were warm, and when you are facing 100-plus temperatures every day, you would do almost anything for some ice.

As I've said, one release was through music. Several guys in the outfit played guitar, and we would run through every song we knew. I can't vouch for the quality of sound we made, but we sure as hell had a good time making it. It didn't matter that we ended up singing a lot of the same songs every night. The potent Vietnamese weed insured that to our ears we made a beautiful noise.

In the late 60s, many young men and women were enjoying cannabis. Those who enlisted or were drafted into the army often continued to partake, just more circumspectly—

naturally, the military tended to frown on this form of recreation. About half the guys didn't partake of marijuana at all. I wasn't heavy into grass, but I enjoyed it from time to time. The unwritten rule was that you didn't use weed anytime you might have to work on the gun.

Ironically, my worst night in Vietnam began with one of those mellow sing-alongs. Perhaps a dozen of us were sitting and singing some Peter, Paul and Mary songs. Someone suggested "The Great Mandala." Copyright issues prevent me from quoting it here, but for me, it's one of the greatest peace songs of all time. It was heart wrenching for me to be sitting in the middle of a war zone, taking part in that war and yet singing that song.

We were about halfway through the song when someone came running up to us to announce an immediate fire mission. By then I was so well trained to scramble to the gun that my body reacted automatically, leaving my brain to catch up. On the one hand, the last thing I wanted to do at that moment was take part in this war. On the other hand, I knew there were likely American soldiers out there in the bush in trouble and needing help. In such cases, you do what you have to do, whatever that is. I felt like I was damned if I did and damned if I didn't. Each man handled those conflicts in his own way. I tried my best to throw myself into the physical exertion that was necessary to work as a part of a well-functioning team. We each did our jobs as expected, but throughout that fire mission I couldn't escape the words of "The Great Mandala" or the brutal contrast between what I was singing and what I was doing.

Luckily, fire missions could sometimes be false alarms.

For example, the army set out listening devices in order to detect enemy movements. When those devices rang, we went into full fighting mode and began to fire our artillery. But even a strong wind could set off the listening devices, making us work like crazy for an hour or more shooting at nothing at all. What's more, we seldom learned if we were firing at something real or imaginary. I suppose that was a blessing in its own way.

I have been forever thankful that, as a member of the artillery, my duty did not force me to see the results of our actions with the gun. But that distance didn't absolve me from a sense of the death and destruction we were causing. An infantryman in the bush may kill or maim numerous enemy during his tour, but the shells we were firing in all likelihood killed and wounded perhaps hundreds more during my time in country. This reality is something that I will always carry with me.

On occasion we would see soldiers back from engagements in the bush. Sometimes they would ask if we had fired the night before. At times they would thank us for the help they so desperately needed. Such is the nature of war.

On a different front there came a change in my relationship, or lack thereof, with TP. When it came to getting along with people, I tried to treat everyone pretty much the same—except for him. He was a special case. I continued to catch his eye and signal hello despite his efforts to ignore me. This had been going on for several weeks when I learned that TP was getting "short," our slang for a tour in Vietnam coming to an end. It wasn't uncommon for a soldier who had made it up to that point without major injury to begin to get a bit nervous. All he had to do was hang in there another month or so and he'd be home free (or, as it was commonly put, "skying up, back to the world"). But all soldiers know that life loves a really good joke. Knowing that anything (read: "something really bad") could happen to them at the last minute, some troops became so paranoid that they dreaded even having to leave the hooch as their time grew shorter. However, superiors expected them to continue to show up for duty. They had to be out there in the middle of a war zone risking their necks hour after hour, day after day, to virtually the last day of their duty.

I watched for TP to grow more and more nervous as the days passed. I have to admit both that I might have been guessing at his feelings and also that he hid them pretty well. But by the time he was down to a couple days, I felt pretty sure that he was a nervous wreck, as so many had been before him. His behavior was jittery and jumpy, increasingly short-tempered and distracted. I noticed people trying to give him a wide berth. Steadfastly, he continued to refuse to acknowledge my positive gestures.

Finally, the day of his departure arrived. It was now only hours before he would be out of this hellhole and on his way back to his pre-army life. I happened to be walking across the compound on my way to the gun just as TP was putting his gear into the back of the army's version of a pickup truck. The sergeant called my name and I stopped to look back. He told me to go get my M-16, flak jacket and helmet and accompany TP on his way back to Quang Tri. I winced when I heard the order. The trip to Quang Tri and back was considerably more dangerous than doing my job at the fire support base. Yes, a minesweeper went over the road from Charlie 2 every morning. But we could still never tell when the Vietcong would want to have target practice at passing trucks or plant another land mine.

The first half of the trip was uneventful as we bumped along the road in the back of the open pickup. I'm sure TP was just as surprised as I was that I had been chosen for this detail. He hadn't spoken to me since the day we met, and it was clear he had nothing to say to me now. We traveled in uncomfortable but mutual silence, sharing that shallow metal foxhole on wheels.

Then we came under fire. When the first few bullets came zinging past us, my outlook instantly changed from cautious concern to full-blown fear. TP's scramble to become as small a target as possible told me he felt the same. The back of a pickup truck doesn't afford a whole lot of protection from shooters at some elevations. Since it's difficult at best to determine the location of a sniper as you're bouncing around back there, I began returning fire in only the most general of directions. TP was unarmed, since he had been required to check in his rifle before leaving Charlie 2. We were both screaming at the driver to step on it and get us the hell out of there, although our requests were purely unnecessary.

In what was probably no more than a minute but felt like eternity, we were out of range of the sniper's fire. I was so filled with adrenaline that my heart rate didn't return to normal immediately, and the look on TP's face told me he was feeling much the same. We rode on in near silence except for some fitting profanity, sitting lower in the back of the truck and with our eyes searching the countryside for anyone else seeking to interrupt our little outing.

When we reached the airport, the driver pulled up next to the tarmac. TP hopped out, and I handed him his gear. As he took his duffel, he looked me in the eye, and with a serious look on his face said, "You take care." These were the first words he had spoken to me since the day we met, and I could see that he meant them. Before I could respond he turned and walked away. I stood there in the back of the truck in shock, watching him leave. I had a crazy mixture of emotions. One was a bittersweet sense that somehow I had finally broken through, but another part of my brain questioned that I really had heard his unexpected words.

Our time together had been scant, our interactions even more so, and I never saw him again. Still, my interactions with TP stand out vividly among my memories of that time in Vietnam. They were proof, in a small way, that I had power over my own reactions—that I didn't have to feel or act hostile just because someone was cold or distrustful of me, and that differences based on something as superficial as skin color didn't have to define a relationship. That "You take care" felt like a small victory for me and, I hope, for him.

A couple weeks later we got a request from the company commander: take all the extra powder packets that were not used during a fire mission and place them around the perimeter of the fire support base. The notion was that, if we were attacked, we could set off the powder and light up the target area in hopes of discouraging the attackers. There was one minor flaw in this plan, as we soon learned. When someone inadvertently set off some of the packets, perhaps with a discarded cigarette, it set one of our tanks on fire. I still have photographs of the tank burning out on our perimeter. At least now we knew that if the enemy attacked with tanks, we could set them ablaze. I wonder if that's been written up in a tactical handbook somewhere.

That wasn't the only job we were given that broke up the routine at the risk of being either pointless or totally counterproductive. Men understood the motivation behind increasing our defenses. Filling sandbags, digging ditches and such made some kind of sense, since we could see how it might increase our safety. But the same couldn't be said of the beautification efforts we were asked to take on when the brass ran out of useful projects: things like painting empty powder canisters and making a row of them around the base of the berms in front of each gun.

Working in 100° weather to build the equivalent of a white picket fence was a task difficult to put your heart into. And the new projects seemed to just keep coming. None of us was happy about the busywork, and we were pretty vocal among each other about just what nonsense it was.

"Did you paint those canisters with polka dots or stripes today?" "Fast Eddie," another one of my buddies on the gun, asked one day.

"Better look out or I'll a paint target on your ass," a buddy named Jimbo replied.

We all agreed that we'd never seen such a waste of time and energy.

Sometimes I could come up with a crazy idea of my own. I've already described the weather. Soaking rains were the norm for four or five months of the year, but one day we got exciting news that we were going to have a really big storm—a monsoon, in Asian terms. We were warned to batten down the hatches and get ready for a major blow. The winds were anticipated to be blowing at about 70 mph and they did not disappoint.

Having never experienced 70 mph winds, I was really curious. Or maybe I was more stupid than curious. At any rate, in the middle of the storm I worked my way out of the hooch and headed up on top of it, crawling on my hands and knees. I carefully stood up and found that I could lean at about a 45° angle and let the wind hold me up. I have no way of knowing how hard it was actually blowing, but I sure would not have wanted it blowing any harder. My curiosity and stupidity both satisfied, I crawled back down to re-enter the hooch. It was only after the storm had passed and the weather had cleared that it became apparent that the high winds had blown sundry parts of the camp to what amounted to an entirely new area code. Any of those parts blowing around could easily have encountered me and knocked my block off. As it was, hundreds if not thousands of dollars of damage had been done. Since the United States Army is seldom short on manpower when it comes to cleaning things up, all was back in working order in no time.

Another special night was July 20, 1969. I was standing in the compound staring up at the moon—just staring at it. Beautiful as always, it was even more mysterious than usual because I had just been told (by one of the sergeants who had access to a military radio) that there were men up there walking on its surface. Apollo 11 had landed. Wow! Amazing! Wouldn't it be great if mankind declared the moon a war-free zone? Coincidentally, it was also my baby sister's sixth birthday. How strange it felt to know that mankind was taking that "giant step" forward on her birthday, and that she and my family had the same moon in their sky that I did in mine, if at a different time.

There was one more unusual event during this period: my appearance before the promotion board. I felt well prepared, and fairly at ease during the session. Afterward, my sergeant told me that I had done better than any of the other men who were up for promotion to corporal. This being the army, of course, action on my promotion would take time even if things went well—and they didn't.

Scary or weird as they could be, these kinds of unusual moments—crazy or profound, dangerous or moving—helped break the monotony of life at Charlie 2. For the most part, each day was pretty much the same as the day that preceded it. The food was the same with minor variations, tasty enough that there were few complaints. The tasks of fire missions were the same. The chores, such as guard duty and KP, were the same. And every night I would sleep through explosions outside and the wanderings of the house rats inside. Nothing ever seemed to change except for experienced guys leaving and new guys arriving.

Sometimes it seemed like things would never change. But that was an illusion. Unbeknownst to me, it was time for something to break loose, and, before long, things shifted.

16

CAN I CATCH A BREAK?

The week after TP left, a truck loaded with projos showed up at Gun 4. This was a good thing, as we were low on ammunition. The shells came banded in sets of three. The task of unloading them fell to whoever was working the projo pit at the time. Housing for them consisted of a wooden base piece with three shallow holes into which each of the projos's bases would fit vertically, and a top wooden piece with three holes that would slide down over the three noses of the projectiles. The top and bottom pieces were then held tightly together with metal bands. The set of three, weighing about 600 pounds, was lowered to the ground by a small crane mounted in the back of the truck. Someone would then cut the metal bands in order to remove the top wooden piece. Then each projo was either moved off its base and rolled away by hand, or was tipped over off the base onto the ground to be stood up and waddle-walked away.

As I was taking part in this ritual that morning, someone tipped over a projo that caught me unprepared. The nose of the 200-pound projectile hit the toe of my boot, with all of its weight focused on that one point. After I hopped around for a couple minutes, I took my boot off to survey the damage. One particular toe had taken the brunt of the blow and was pretty well smashed.

I caught a ride to see the doctor in Dong Ha. The office was nothing to shout about. Part of a larger medical facility, it was two rooms, bare bones, utilitarian, and protected with sand bags. But I hadn't expected anything fancy in a war zone. The doctor cleaned up my toe and told me there was nothing much he could do, it would do no good to splint it, and I would be walking with crutches for a while. I don't know if you've ever heard of a "million-dollar wound"—the phrase describing an injury that sends you back home and out of the service. Mine was more like a $49.95 wound. It's virtually impossible to haul a 200-pound projectile to the back of a waiting cannon while walking with crutches in mud and gravel. With my injury and crutches, I could only manage to deliver the separate loading powder pack to the gun. Crutches or no, the powder pit is a much cushier job than that of humping projos. It might not have gotten me out of active duty but, trust me, it was a good change.

I enjoyed my "lucky break" for a week or ten days. As my toe healed and the pain subsided, I began to feel guilty regarding the fellow I had displaced from the powder pit (who had naturally been moved back down to the projo pit). I must admit that I let a few days in which I could have returned to humping joes go by. Then fate, or whatever, stuck its nose in again and nudged me back on the straight and narrow. It was Sunday morning and, for the first time in some weeks, a minister was on the base to hold service in Gun 3's powder pit. A number of us from various guns gathered there and the service began. Of course, there were no chairs, let alone pews, so everyone was standing.

Little more than halfway through, we all heard a familiar, unwelcome sound. Eyes grew large, heads turned quickly, and brains and bodies reacted to the screaming whistle of an incoming rocket. Believe me, a powder pit is the last place any of us wanted to be when explosive devices were aimed our way. The pit emptied in split seconds, with men running in every direction. It didn't take me more than a few steps to realize that my crutches were more of a hindrance than a help. Prudently, I left them in the dust, so to speak. Near Gun 4 we had dug a ditch—open at both ends, wide and deep enough to hold a good-sized piece of pipe, and covered with the inevitable sand bags—as a kind of personnel shelter large enough for several men to crawl into. Three other men from our gun joined me in sprinting across 40 yards of open terrain. It didn't strike me until I was entering one end of the pipe that, along with my crutches, I had pretty much left my comrades in the dust too, despite the fact that I was supposed to be a gimp. Clearly, the jig was up. Busted. Back to the salt mines of the projo pit.

After I had been in country about four months, a couple months after my foot injury, I received a letter from my mother that was destined to change the course of things for me. When I first read it, I was shocked. My brain went reeling while I tried to wrap my mind around it. By that evening I felt I had to share this letter with someone I trusted. Tom immediately came to mind. By this time it was dark, so I grabbed him. We took our flashlights to a metal storage shed, where I read him the letter.

As I've mentioned before, numerous people had sought out my mother for spiritual guidance over the years. Recently, she had been mentioning the difficult time she was having trying to help a particular woman. In desperation, Mom decided to try to contact her spiritual mentor, David—as I've also said, he had died some years earlier. Before he passed on, he had told her that if she ever needed him, she would be able to contact him. Her letter told me that she had reached out and made contact with someone or something. The use of language and no-nonsense approach among other things convinced her it was David. After she asked for guidance on the woman she was helping, she asked David about me. Had she been wrong to tell me that I could be spared the experience of the war through prayer if I didn't feel right about the war and my participation in it? He said, "You were wrong. There was karma, but it is paid now." He didn't make any specific predictions; he said only that my karma had been paid, and that therefore I should not have to stay in Vietnam much longer.

I finished reading the letter to Tom, and we sat there staring at each other. I'm sure Tom didn't know what to think. I was excited and confused. My trust in both David and my mother made me take David's "news" very seriously. On the one hand, I was thrilled at the thought of going home. On the other hand, I couldn't imagine such a thing happening short of me being injured in some serious way—in which case, I might get home but it wouldn't really feel much like I was released from either karma or the war!

Still, I believed what my mother's letter told me: that I had

*** 2ᴮ ***

This I hesitate to tell you. It sounds so far out. Phyllis has an XX Ouija Board. I have always been able to cause it to work ....that is, it will move for me when it will not move for others. However, I can also make it say whatever I wish it to by my will....so I mostly stay away from it. I could never trust what came over it......

However, the other night, or rather, early morning.....Phyllis was having a terrible time. She was at a point of rebellion with me. She had to have help. So, recalling that David had promised that I had only to call on him and he would be with me, I meditated on his face.....as well as I could recall it.. .....told Phyllis to get her board.....and I asked David to speak to me.

I would not consider doing this for myself......you understand.

I am sure it was he who came through. There was none of the usual foolishness .....it was slow at first.....then he spelled out...."The Ouija is new to me."

He was his old arbitrary self. No nonsense. He spelled it out for her. Much what I had been saying.....but in his own words.

One time another force seemed to be pushing its way through. I spoke sharply saying....."Get out. I will speak to no one but David tonight." I could almost hear him chuckle as the board spelled "Get Ruth!" At the time of his death I was a real door mat in every way. I felt his pleasure at the change.

In among her questions every so often he would direct an unexpected comment to me. "Tell Ruth that I find her very shiney." (He XXXXXX meant, I presume - that the Light is coming through my Aura better.) Again, he said, "You have made very good progress." Later again, "You have only a few more lives to go. Does that make you happy, Ruth?"

I asked him about a personal problem. He said "You need not live tomorrow's work today. You will be strong, beautiful and very happy."

I asked him if I had been wrong about your not having to XX go to Viet Nam & engage in killing if you identified with Christ within. He said "You were wrong. There was Karma but it is paid now." I asked him why you had to go...."He knows." he answered. *Subconsciously? Otherwise?*

As ever he would give no specific predictions.....saying only that your Karma has been paid now.....& indicating that therefore you should not have to stay there much longer.

Phyllis' eyes were so bad she couldn't follow the words so I know she was not influencing it....and he deliberately changed the wording of his statements when I anticipated them....the meaning would be the same....but I would not know which letter was coming first or next.... I presume that this was to be a reassurance to me later that I had not made the board say what I wanted it to say.

Mostly he said what he wanted to say without questioning on our part. However he did answer a question that has bothered me for years. I asked him why - the last time I saw him that he was so cold to me. It really hurt me xx deeply.

He said...."It was a cutting off lest there be Karma." (Meaning, I presume, lest I put too much emphasis on David as opposed to Principle.)

Ruth in the late 1970s

learned whatever lesson was necessary and that my time at war could rapidly come to an end. I spent some time with Tom batting around the ways I could make that happen immediately, but I kept ending up with the same realization. Much as I wanted to be with MaryAnne, if I stayed where I was for another five months, I would be done with the army and free to lead my own life once again. It was tempting to want to do something now, but trying to manipulate the situation for a faster release didn't make sense. If I was indeed to go home earlier, I needed to trust that the way would reveal itself. At the same time, I was inwardly making a definite choice to leave.

Sitting with Tom, I tried to accept that I might be left in suspense for a while. Something I could not control was happening, it could change my life dramatically, and I might soon be going home. It was hard not to rush back to the hooch and yell out the good news. Instead, I put the letter back in its envelope, stuck it in my pocket, and went on with life in country as usual. Tom, I'm pleased to say, seemed to understand my thinking. He may have thought I was nuts, but he was a good friend and offered his support.

17

FROM THE HILL OF THE ANGELS

Word came down that we were going to "march order." March order is the artillery's term for moving from one place to another. We were told that the place we were moving to was Fire Support Base A-4, or Alpha 4. The Vietnamese had already named this area Con Thien, the English translation of which is "hill of the angels." The name seemed ironic. Con Thien was even closer to the DMZ than Charlie 2. We would be just a fraction of a mile from the demilitarized zone.

Everything had to go except the buildings. It took some time and a great deal of exertion to pack it all up. Eventually, in mid-October, the move came. I was still the designated driver of the gun; up until this time a purely titular role, this now gave me my first chance to actually drive an 8-inch, self-propelled heavy howitzer M-110. I was excited to finally get in the driver's seat. I'm pleased to say that I avoided any major mishaps along the way. I didn't damage army property and, particularly, didn't run over any of my buddies. (The army really frowns on that.)

For some reason, everyone called Fire Support Base A-4

"Con Thien" rather than using its military nickname, as we had at Charlie 2. Fire Support Base A-4 was definitely not an improvement over Charlie 2, whatever you called it, but my fortunes were about to take a turn for the better. To this day I'm not sure what happened. I only know that first, my intentions shifted—and then life itself seemed to follow along.

Up until then, the only U.S. military to populate this area had been the Marines. Nothing personal, but the living standards of the Marine artillery were what I can only describe as somewhat rougher than that of the army. Our company would be putting in a lot of overtime in order to bring it up to the army's standards. Don't get me wrong. I had the greatest respect for the Marines. There was nobody you would rather have with you in a fight. But they existed in what you might say is a different culture. Their focus was more on rapid reactions and quick strikes, where the army tended to put more emphasis on creating infrastructure from which to operate. Anyway, in addition to handling the usual artillery-fire missions, we would need to upgrade and maintain the base.

Some of us called Con Thien the "Mud Hole at the DMZ," adding a wide variety of the most unpleasant modifiers that we could come up with. Battling all that mud into submission was going to take a mighty effort on our part. Our schedules changed from 12 hours on and 12 off to 36 on and 12 off. This was not happy news. It meant that not only were we required to put in a full shift manning the gun, we also had plenty of extra hours to work on the niceties, such as installing a floor in the projo pit (so we didn't have to roll projectiles around in the mud) or building enough bunks (so that we didn't have to roll someone out of our shared beds in order to get some sleep). It was exhausting, and the heat didn't help. We generally tried to get much work done in the morning before it got too hot, and also tried to fit in what we could between the frequent downpours.

War has such a rude habit of interrupting sleep. The shortage of bunks made getting rest difficult but happily, at night on the gun we could at least try to catch a nap in between fire missions. At Con Thien, just like at Charlie 2, we spent some free time catching up on our rest. After that, when there was time off left over, we put it to other good uses, such as poker games. Most of my meager private's pay was going home to MaryAnne, since all my basic needs were being taken care of by the army: three square meals, a uniform, and a bunk with the latest in mosquito netting. When I started playing poker with a group of guys, I tended to come out ahead most evenings. This wasn't due to me being a great poker player, but rather because their skills were even worse than mine. We didn't play for much money, but little by little my winnings added up.

I also developed an interest in learning the guitar. Tom, Steve Bogacki and the other guitar players clearly inspired me. I would sit and watch and listen to them, marveling at their dexterity and their command of the instruments. I started tucking some of my winnings away in hopes of getting enough together to buy a guitar of my own.

There were no guitars for sale near Con Thien, needless to say. You would have to find one on R&R, which in order to be both restful and recreational was necessarily somewhere well away from the war. I figured I would be going on R&R eventually and, of course, the place I wanted to go to was

Hawaii. But as I had explained to MaryAnne in a letter, the chances of that were unlikely in the extreme. Hawaii was the only place you were likely to be able to meet up with your wife or girlfriend, and also the only R&R destination that let you get back to some part of the United States. R&R there being so highly sought after, very few below the rank of sergeant ever got it.

It didn't seem fair, but there was nothing to be done. I would have to settle for Bangkok, Sydney or some such. One of my pals, Ed, had gone to Bangkok and seemed to think it was a lot of fun. Tom, who was planning on heading for Sydney, offered to buy me a guitar while he was there. I started giving him my poker winnings in case my luck changed and I lost what stash I had so far acquired. Eventually, Tom did make it to Australia and brought me back a nice guitar. He was just beginning to teach me how to play it when life took another twist.

I suppose my emotions had been building up for months. The daily grind was wearing me down. I couldn't help but think about MaryAnne, who had finally got around to telling me about a car accident she had been in. Someone had T-boned our sweet, sporty 1967 Toyota Corona. It hadn't been her fault, and she wasn't injured at all, but I'm pretty sure car accidents are not doctor-recommended when you're only five feet tall and several months pregnant. More and more it was clear to me that if there was any way for me to be present at my child's birth, that was where I should be. I still didn't know how to make it happen or if it was even in my control, but I never doubted my mother's message that my "debt" had been paid.

In letters, I learned that my mother was still reading MaryAnne's cards every week. MaryAnne had been making the same wish every time: that "Don and I will be together for the birth of our child." Up until then the answer had consistently been yes, but one day the answer changed. The cards now read that it would be up to MaryAnne; it would be her choice. As with David's message about my time in Vietnam, this puzzled me a little. Practically speaking, how could she make this happen? Yet again, I had to accept that the "how" of these predictions wouldn't be clear for a while.

One evening after being at Con Thien a month or so, I was coming off the gun, done with my 36-hour shift. I was in a lousy mood and really tired. I went to my hooch and rolled the guy who was sharing my bunk out of it. I lay down, and, after a few moments of gathering my thoughts, said to whomever that ultimate power is, "Okay, that's it. I'm finished. I want to go home." That was my prayer. Then I went to sleep.

Life went on as usual for the next three days. Then, on a hot afternoon (what's new?) word came down that there was a battery formation happening immediately. Formations are very rare in war zones. The army generally does not like to have all its personnel making an easy target in a formation's straight columns and rows. The troops were looking around with questioning expressions; I'm sure all of us were trying to think of a reason why the formation was necessary.

The first sergeant stepped up and began to speak. Explaining that another sergeant had decided not to use his Hawaii R&R because he didn't want to spend the money, he asked, "Is there anyone who would like an R&R to Hawaii?" I shot my hand in the air, assuming that all the others were doing the same.

As I turned my head and looked around to see how many others were competing for the spot, I was shocked. I was the only one with my hand in the air. This could not be! The first sergeant said, "Graham, do you have the money?" When I said yes, I was sent off to "See the company clerk to start the paperwork."

And there it was. I was going to see my wife! I was beside myself. To this day I'm still dumbfounded by the fact that out of more than 50 men, no one else raised his hand. In my mind it defies explanation, at least on a rational or material level. Was it possible that the angels that helped give Con Thien its Vietnamese name were actually on the job? I was feeling pretty blessed.

The leave was for a week, but a couple days were spent in transit. The plane would leave in three days. Cell phones had not yet been invented, and since letters took at least a week to arrive, writing would be futile. I had no way to let MaryAnne know that I was heading for Honolulu and that she needed to get there pronto. I would have to wait until I arrived in Hawaii, call her from there, and then wait for her to pack, buy a ticket and catch a plane. Despite such logistical problems, needless to say, I was walking on clouds for the next couple days, chomping at the bit to get on that plane to paradise.

18

NEXT STOP, PARADISE

At some point, the hours—or even days—with MaryAnne that would be lost for no good reason except the fact that I couldn't contact her began to torment me. I would be sitting in beautiful Hawaii, doing nothing more than waiting—waiting for my bride to pack, waiting for her to make the trip there to join me. Such a delay now feeling unacceptable, I devised a plan that was definitely risky, and basically foolish as well. But fools rush in where angels fear to even tippy-toe, let alone tread.

The plan was this: I would add a leg to the trip, spending time with MaryAnne in California before returning to Hawaii and from there to Vietnam. Doing this without the army's permission was going AWOL, or absent without leave. The military punishes even brief infractions of this kind with harsh penalties, including confinement and loss of pay. That led to the second part of my plan: I would borrow the fake ID that Danny, one of the guys in my squad, already possessed. I don't know how Dan (who wasn't yet 21 and probably used it for drinking) got a driver's license that identified him as

James Simpson. But happily, Danny, "James Simpson" and I all had the same height, weight and eye color.

I couldn't have gotten away with a stunt like this today, but that was a very different era in travel. Driver's licenses as yet had no photos on them and decades before 9/11, airport security was minimal compared to what we see currently. It was a simpler, more trusting time, in which the person checking you through was an airline employee, not a government worker. I didn't have to go through a metal detector; they didn't ask me to remove my shoes; I don't even remember them x-raying anyone's bag.

So the plan unfolded, with me pushing the risk to the back of my mind. Making sure that I had a civilian suitcase and clothing to match my non-military ID, I hopped in the back of the transport truck that would take me to Dong Ha. It had a tiny airport, the first of three stages I would have to endure. The guys I met along the way were mostly headed to R&R as well, though not necessarily bound for Hawaii. Everyone was smiling and in a good mood, especially the crowd headed for Hawaii. It was a fun flight with plenty of laughter.

Getting to Honolulu in the morning, we were quickly shuffled onto a bus and taken downtown to something akin to an assembly hall. Once we were seated, an army lieutenant took the small stage and began explaining the dos and don'ts of R&R. As you might expect, there were a whole lot of things on the "do not do" list when it came to R&R. Number one, and stressed more than any other, was the fact that we were not permitted to leave Hawaii and go to the continental United States. That being an absolute no-no, anyone guilty of doing so would be duly punished. He continued on down the list of other forbidden actions before citing a laundry list of general information that GIs should know: "Don't drink too much"; "Don't get into fights"; "Treat people with respect while here in Honolulu." Eventually, he finished and we were dismissed. I got up from my chair, walked to the back of the room, picked up my bag and headed for the street. There I flagged down a cab, got in and told the driver, "Take me to the airport."

There the plot thickens and the dangerous part of my plan began. When I got to the airport, I headed for the men's room and entered a stall. I was already wearing civilian clothes, so I used this opportunity to put my military ID in my shoe. Thank goodness, the army didn't require its troops to maintain GI haircuts in Vietnam. In an era where long hair was common for young men, that would have been a dead giveaway.

Once finished in the bathroom, I headed for the ticket agent, using the fake ID to purchase my plane ticket to San Francisco. It was fortunate for me that Honolulu has a warm climate, because I may have been perspiring a bit.

After I got my ticket and knew what time I would be arriving in San Francisco, I went to the phone and called Mary-Anne's brother Joe, who was going to medical school at the University of California at San Francisco. I had known Joe since the Boy Scouts. He was my brother-in-law and had been my best man at the wedding. It would be an understatement to say he was surprised to get a call from me. The conversation went something like this:

"Hello?"

"Joe, this is Don."

Silence. (But I could almost hear the wheels turning).

"Don Graham. Your brother-in-law."

"Don? Where are you?"

"I'm in Honolulu, waiting to catch a plane to San Francisco. I need you to pick me up at the airport, and I need to borrow a car so I can get to Napa. My plane arrives at 3:45. I want to surprise MaryAnne. Can you help me?"

"Yes, I can make that work, and I'll let my folks know to make sure she's at home."

"Great, Joe. Thanks a million. I'll be on United Airlines flight 457."

Naturally enough, Joe wanted to know what was going on, so I briefly explained the situation. All he could say was, "Graham, you are one crazy galoot!"

Waiting at the gate for my flight to San Francisco, I was nervous as hell. The minutes passed too slowly, and it seemed to take forever to get on that plane. I kept waiting for the military police to walk through the gate and ask to see my orders, but it never happened. Finally, we boarded. Then five more hours of torture sitting in the plane. Eventually, we arrived in San Francisco. Joe was there waiting, and I had never been so glad to see him.

After I dropped him off at his apartment in San Francisco, I headed for Napa to see my pregnant bride. It's a good thing I was driving a Volkswagen Bug that was incapable of going as fast as I wanted it to. Otherwise, I would've been stopped multiple times for speeding.

At the Pramuk house, Greg, one of MaryAnne's younger brothers, answered my knock and told me in hushed tones that she was resting. I tiptoed down the hall to her bedroom, slowly twisted the doorknob and opened the door just a crack. I said, "Has anyone seen my sweetheart? "

I will never forget the look on that wonderful face of hers. Eyes wide! Mouth agape! And totally incapable of saying one single word. Suffice it to say the next couple minutes were filled with a lot of hugging and kissing, then staring at each other, and then more hugging and kissing.

"How in the world did you get here?" she was finally able to ask.

"Well, I took a truck, several plane rides and the VW I swiped from your brother."

"I mean, why are you here?"

"I couldn't wait to see you."

"You crazy idiot! I thought there was no way you could get an R&R to the USA!"

"Things sort of worked out. I'll explain later."

As I looked at my sweetheart, there was no mistaking that she was six months pregnant. She was more beautiful than ever. But I must admit that although I had seen photos, the reality truly hit home at that moment. There really was a child on the way, and our lives would be forever changed. Priorities were already reshuffling in my head. Things that seemed important moments ago had quickly faded to the background. I asked MaryAnne how she was feeling. She said she was feeling good, that it seemed she was having a fairly easy pregnancy. I was speechless. I could do nothing but sit and stare, marveling at the fact that we were suddenly together again and realizing that every passing moment with her was precious and irreplaceable.

Finally coming down from the clouds and recognizing that there might be other people in the vicinity who would like to be included in this happy moment, we went out to join the rest of the family. It was a happy gathering, with her brothers and sisters asking numerous questions. I didn't want to advertise to the young ones that I was breaking the law to be there. I couched my answers in generalities that made it sound like a normal leave from the army. It felt so wonderful to be home but also bittersweet, knowing as I did that I only had a few days.

After visiting with family for a while, we took the five-minute drive to my folks' house to include them in the homecoming festivities. They had been warned that I was coming, so some of the shock had worn off. They were all very happy to see me, especially my mother and my baby sister, Mary. Only five years old, Mary again spent a lot of time sitting on my lap. My brothers Mark and Paul were 15 and 13 at the time, and it was great to see them too. Some soldiers love to glorify their military days. In my mind there was nothing the least bit glorious about what was going on in Vietnam, and I certainly didn't want my brothers thinking there was. I responded to their many questions as humbly as I could, with little effort required. At that moment Vietnam seemed like a bad dream. I didn't want to think about it, I just wanted to appreciate this precious time. I would have liked to talk to Mom about Vietnam and David's message, but in all the bustle we didn't get a quiet moment.

That evening MaryAnne and I drove out to the mini-ranch, where we planned to spend the week that I was home. It was a wonderful evening. Neither one of us could stop grinning. We stayed up late and slept late and thought we were dreaming the whole time.

19

WHAT'S UP, DOC?

I awoke the next morning with a pain in my back. At first I tried to ignore it but as the day went on, the pain strengthened. I got sick to my stomach several times. At other times the pain would let up and it seemed like I was improving. But if anything, by that afternoon I was feeling worse. I couldn't believe I was being forced to waste this precious time lying in bed, and the growing worry that I might have a serious illness while AWOL made my discomfort worse. I made it through the night, but by the next morning MaryAnne decided it was best to call my mother and have her come out to the house.

We had told no one other than our immediate families that I was here, but now we didn't really have a choice. MaryAnne and Mom decided to take me to see our longtime—and much trusted—family doctor in Vallejo. Dr. Elston had been my doctor since I was an infant. Now in his 60s, he had been bald for as long as I'd known him. He still had a semi-halo of hair, though it had resolutely turned white over the years. He greeted me with "Hello, Ronnie." All my life he had called me Ronnie for reasons unknown. I had never felt the need to correct him, nor was I about to start at this late date.

He checked me over and said, "Ron, I'm going to put you in the hospital. You have kidney stones."

I looked at him, weighed my options and admitted the truth. "Doc, I can't do that. I'm not even supposed to be in the continental United States."

He didn't seem the least bit concerned regarding this illegality of mine. Without missing a beat, he said, "Well, you still need to be in the hospital."

Disbelieving, I realized that I was stuck between a rock and a hard place. The rock was a kidney stone and the hard place was a hospital. A hospital in Honolulu, no less, since I certainly couldn't risk getting stuck in one in California. I was angry as hell, but I had little choice, since I was sick as hell too.

"I guess I'm going back to Hawaii," I said.

By 5 o'clock that evening MaryAnne, my mother and I were back at the San Francisco International Airport with the regrettable goal of purchasing a ticket to return to Honolulu.

After I got my ticket (using the same fake ID) I felt my current condition insisting that I take a restroom break, now! MaryAnne and Mom waited in the vicinity. When I came out, I looked around but didn't immediately see them. Since boarding time was getting close, I thought perhaps they had gone to the boarding area. There was no sign of them at the gate either. I waited as long as I could, but finally had to board.

I later learned that they had been waiting near the men's room and had never seen me come out. They eventually sent another fellow in there looking for me, of course to no avail.

By the time they got to the gate, the plane was already taking off. They didn't know if I had made it in time or not. Their first attempts to find out if I was on the plane were unsuccessful, but they kept on until airport personnel agreed to check on an ailing passenger. That was how they learned that I had indeed boarded, which, needless to say, relieved their minds. Meanwhile, I was beyond miserable, having left my wife after less than 48 hours, heading now for a solitary R&R with kidney stones as company. The best laid plans....

I can't say the flight to Honolulu was enjoyable. To be with my wife for so few hours and then have to leave so suddenly was horrible. And then there was the matter of the pain in my side. (For those unfamiliar with kidney stones, the pain of passing a stone is generally compared to that of childbirth without anesthesia. I obviously can't speak from experience on that, but I can say the pain was agonizing.) I held my side for five hours during the flight and took some painkillers, but didn't find much relief at all.

When we reached Honolulu, I made my way to the R&R information booth at the airport. There were so many GIs coming and going during the Vietnam War that the government had created an R&R Information Center right there in the airport. I asked one of the fellows behind the counter where a GI should go if he was sick. The answer was Tripler Army Medical Center—the army's primary military hospital complex in the Pacific, as well as its largest. The bad news, he told me, was that the hospital lay out of town and up on a hill. It took a $10 cab ride to get there, a lot for a cab ride in 1969. I didn't see that I had much choice, so I flagged a cab and told him to take me to Tripler.

Because it was night, I couldn't see much, nor was I in any kind of mood for sightseeing. I have no idea how long that ride was. I was too lost in my own discomfort to notice. Eventually the cab dropped me off at the lighted sign that said "Emergency Room." I entered a large room with many chairs and a long counter with several service windows. I did what soldiers do and got in line. When I got to the front of the line, the uniformed GI behind the counter, sporting a military haircut and wearing horn-rimmed glasses, asked why I was there. I told him I had kidney stones. He asked me how I knew I had kidney stones. This caught me off guard. I had to think quickly. I said my father had kidney stones and I knew the symptoms. He seemed to accept that. He gave me a piece of paper and told me to sit over in a section to the left where a dozen other members of the military were already waiting to be seen.

When I was finally called into the stark examination room, I was quite surprised by the doctor who walked in the door. Unlike every other doctor I'd encountered in the army, this one wasn't male, and she was probably only a couple years older than I was. I wasn't against female doctors in any way but I had never been seen by one, so I was finding it a little strange.

After she had finished her exam and I had provided a urine sample, I asked, "What part of the hospital will I be in?"

She responded, "Oh, I don't know if they even admit patients with your symptoms."

This blew my mind. I thought, *I bought a ticket and flew for five hours away from friends and family just so I could go downtown and roll around in pain in a hotel room, alone?*

Looking back, I realize that her comment probably came from the fact that faced with heading back to war, all too many soldiers went to the hospital with medical complaints (real and, probably, less so) they hoped would keep them from having to return to their unit, if only temporarily. Ultimately, she did admit me to the hospital. I ended up in a very large and very clean urology ward with somewhere between 30 to 40 hospital beds, most of which were currently occupied, in nice neat rows. The space was totally devoid of anything akin to privacy curtains. Maybe the military figured that since there was no privacy in a barracks, there didn't need to be any in a hospital, either. We were just one big happy family. Well, maybe not all that happy. I, for one, was totally bummed out. I was in pain, not sure what would need to be done to get me out of pain, and spending the R&R I had been so lucky to get in a hospital. Worst of all, my wife was 2,400 miles away.

Halfway through the morning I heard a sound that I thought was an incoming rocket. Before I knew it, I was in full self-preservation mode—under my bed. It was an automatic move intended to keep me alive in a war zone. Looking around, I realized that none of the guys around me had reacted as I had. Nor had they said a word. They just behaved like nothing had happened. It would take me a while to get over those reactions of mine. Right then I felt a little foolish, but the good news was that at that moment I was feeling no pain. I'll take feeling foolish over kidney-stone pain every time.

One of the curious qualities of kidney stones is that the pain veers between being "on" or "off" depending on the movement of the stone, or stones. If a stone—which has sharp, crystalline edges and, as its name suggests, is very hard—blocks the normal urinary pathway, the pain can be fierce; if not, you can feel fine, at least for a while. But look out, here it would come again. I hadn't a single doubt in the world that a small, humble stone could have brought down better men than me.

Pain or no pain, MaryAnne and I found opportunities to talk daily. There were of course no cell phones, as I've said, and the military didn't feel it necessary to provide individual bedside phones for its patients. My calls were always made via the hospital's patient pay phone, which required me to reverse all charges. Since MaryAnne knew the number, she would frequently take a turn being the caller. Long-distance and collect calls were expensive, and these ended up on her parents' bill. We decided we needed to pay for them, though we didn't know exactly how much expense we were racking up yet. But the calls were beyond value to both of us, they would end when I was back in Vietnam, and it seemed to us that they were worth every cent.

Much of our conversation had to do with whether or not MaryAnne was going to come to Hawaii to have the baby. The cards were still reading that whether we would be together for the birth would be MaryAnne's choice, but the bottom line was that we didn't know whether I would be returned to Vietnam in the near future. It was possible that I could pass a kidney stone or two soon, and then be judged ready to resume my military duties.

The doctors kept running one test after another. The results showed that in addition to having kidney stones, half of my left kidney wasn't functioning. I had become a diagnostic curiosity. The medical staff stuck me with sundry probes, inserted various tubes wherever they felt necessary, and channeled fluids into every orifice they could find. In what was soon a familiar routine, a doctor would come to tell me something about the next test they were going to be running on me. I would then ask whether I was going to be awake, and the doctor would say, "Yes, but we'll give you something. You'll feel so good you won't care one way or the other what we are doing." I do recall lying on the table once with medical people around me, feeling so good that I was asking them if they had ever smoked weed. Had I been in full control of my senses, no such question would ever have occurred to me, but I'm sure I wasn't the first GI who wondered.

Eventually, they narrowed down the cause of my kidney malfunction to three possibilities: cancer, tuberculosis and a congenital defect. I said, "I'll take C." The plan was to go in and take the non-functioning half kidney out in what's called a hemi-nephrectomy. The doctor said, "If things don't go well, we might have to take the entire kidney, but that's not a problem because you have another one." I lay there thinking, *Yeah, it sounds pretty easy to take half my kidneys. Bet it wouldn't sound so easy if it was half your kidneys.*

20

TWENTY QUESTIONS

A key topic of conversation between MaryAnne and myself had recently been whether she should come to Honolulu. I would always argue in favor of her staying right where she was. My logic went as follows: she was living with her parents, with a father who was a physician; the house was located a few blocks from the hospital; and since she was in a home with numerous brothers and sisters, there would always be someone around to help. In addition, it was possible that the army would patch me up quickly and send me back to Vietnam at the same time she was heading for Hawaii. The very thought of her stuck there without me was nerve-wracking.

Her reasoning, on the other hand, went something like this: "I am coming to Honolulu. We will be together when the baby is born." End of argument.

I held my resolve pretty well up until the time when they set the date for my operation. Then the conversation between us went something like this:

MaryAnne: "I'm coming."

Me: "No, you're not."
MaryAnne: "Yes, I am."
Me: "No, you're not."
MaryAnne: "Yes, I am."

At some point, I realized that further argument was futile. She had a will of her own and a checking account, and I had no way to stop her. The big, powerful warrior was soundly defeated by his woman. So I did what any big, powerful guy who wears the pants in the family would do in the face of imminent defeat: I called her back and told her to come ahead. The date of my operation was so close that the doctor graciously decided to delay the procedure by three days to make sure MaryAnne could get there in time.

At the same time that MaryAnne and I were debating her journey, her dad was lobbying for me to go to the psychology department in the hospital and ask for a job. It hadn't even occurred to me that the hospital had a psychology department; even when I finally accepted that such a department might exist, I was of the firm belief that they sure as hell would not be giving me a job. I mean, really...taking someone with a degree in psychology away from the artillery and re-assigning him to a job in psychology? That would make actual sense, and I had seen no evidence of common sense since joining the army. Besides, I was facing surgery and had no clue about when I would be fit again. However, my father-in-law and MaryAnne were relentless. Eventually I gave in and agreed to make a visit. But I can't say that I really believed anything would come of it.

Imagine my surprise when I was given an appointment for an interview in the Psychology Service! Perhaps there was a chance after all—albeit a very slim one. Why, if this were to work out....*No!* I admonished myself. I couldn't allow myself to start fantasizing about anything so unlikely. But I also couldn't stop myself from wishing. Getting a job at Tripler could lay the groundwork for a truly productive and rewarding future and mean the fulfillment of all those dreams of helping others that got me started in the field of psychology in the first place. And of course, it could mean a transfer that would get me out of Vietnam, and reunited with MaryAnne, for good. Clearly, it was a shot I had to take. If I didn't, I'd be second-guessing myself for years to come.

There was a lot at stake. When I showed up for the job interview, I was quite nervous. In the comfortable waiting room decorated in an island motif, I took a few deep breaths and tried to be calm. Within a few minutes I was met by Bob and David, two psychology techs. Both were dressed in standard khaki army uniforms, with all the standard patches, insignias and rank indications. Bob was tall and lean with a mop of blond hair combed to one side. David was a handsome young Asian, probably Japanese. I explained that I had come from Vietnam and had no resumé or academic records with me. That didn't seem to concern them. They then introduced me to Dr. Sidney Halperin, head of the Psychology Service. Both of the psych techs sat in on the interview. That, in and of itself, told me something important about Dr. Halperin. His interest in the perceptions and opinions of his assistants was a sign that he trusted and valued those who worked for him.

Unlike Bob and David, Dr. Halperin was a civilian, something I could see immediately from his lack of a military uniform. He was small in stature—perhaps five feet seven or so—and clean-shaven, with gray hair neatly combed and somewhat sharp facial features. He wore a suit and tie and well-polished shoes. In his early 70s by this time, he had been the head of psychology at Tripler since the 1950s, when Hawaii was still just a territory of the United States. Later, I learned that he was an avid tennis buff who loved great painters and their art. He had a pet peeve that he made no effort to conceal: those "sociopaths" who frequently parked in his reserved spot. He also didn't care much for social workers. He was proud to note that he was the last civilian head of a psychology department anywhere in the United States Army.

That day, Dr. Halperin explained that the Psychology Service existed to provide psychological testing rather than therapy. (Clinical and therapeutic treatment would be done in the Department of Psychiatry.) Were I to work there, my position would focus mainly on administering and scoring psychological examinations and assessments. After some questions about my academic background, he explained the department's need.

"It just so happens that David is due to get out of the army shortly," he said. "So I need to know what your situation is in regards to availability."

Much as I found myself wanting the job, I had no choice but to be candid. "I'm due to have an operation a few days from now. I believe I could be available for duty within a couple weeks after the operation."

Of course, I had no way of knowing how such a transfer could be achieved or if it was even possible. But the "fate train" I was on was rolling down the track and I was determined to ride it to the end of the line. For the first time, I could really see David's prediction coming true. Here, in a form I couldn't have imagined even a week or two before, was a possible means of leaving Vietnam early and without injury.

Dr. Halperin asked me to wait in the outer office while he and his technicians conferred. Within four or five minutes they called me back in. "Don," Dr. Halperin said, "we would be very pleased to have you join our staff here in Psychology."

This would mean an assignment to Tripler until my exit from the military. You can imagine my excitement! I was shaking everyone's hand in the room. This was a dream come true! A part of me doubted that this could be happening.

Even better, when I asked about my deployment in Vietnam, Dr. Halperin said it wasn't a problem. "We'll send through some transfer papers and it will all be taken care of."

Dr. Halperin's boss, in turned out, was a colonel who reported to a general. If the hospital said I was needed in Hawaii, no one in Vietnam was going to argue. GIs like myself were just cogs in the war machine; if my particular cog was needed elsewhere, there would be no objection.

All of what had preceded and all that might very well follow: it was beyond my powers of belief. Not only was I not going back to Vietnam, I was going to spend the next year in paradise with MaryAnne and our soon-to-be-delivered child. Almost as good, I would be working under a civilian, doing psychological testing that could only help advance my career. It meant that MaryAnne and I would be together not just for the birth of the child but also for the duration of my time in the army and far beyond. How can this be happening? I kept thinking.

I floated back to the ward to share my good fortune with my fellow patients and, of course, immediately got on the phone with MaryAnne, running up that bill some more! We were both half-delirious with joy. We were both struck with the realization that multiple predictions seemed to be coming true. David's message had suggested that I would get out of Vietnam early, Elsie had predicted that I would stay on an island, and MaryAnne was a driving force in the fact that we would be together for the birth of our child. What was happening wasn't unexpected, but the way it was occurring was, and it left us in a state of wonder and gratitude.

Meanwhile, there was surgery to contend with. MaryAnne arrived in Honolulu a couple days after the interview. A male nurse on the staff was kind enough to take me to the airport to meet her. She was even more visibly pregnant, and more beautiful, than the last time I had seen her—she had what I could only term a radiance about her. We checked her in to the hospital's guesthouse, which had a number of bedrooms for family members of the hospital's patients. She was able to stay there while I was being treated, and there was no charge since I was now an incoming member of Tripler's staff. This being a totally unexpected windfall, again we felt blessed.

Once I'd gotten MaryAnne settled in her guestroom, she and I went to the maternity department to get her registered and scheduled for an exam.

During the following three weeks, she spent a whole lot of time sitting next to my bed on the urology ward. She also took me on walks so that I could get some exercise. Having been separated for so long, and with so many new and novel experiences lying ahead for the two of us, we never seemed to run out of things to talk about.

At some point MaryAnne brought up our phone bill. All those phone conversations we'd engaged in between Honolulu and Napa had generated a bill in excess of $300. A normal phone bill at this time would have been in the range of $10 and as I've said, the rent on the mini-ranch was only $35 a month. There was no way I was going to let that bill get paid by my in-laws. I called my stepfather in Napa and asked him to sell the 1962 Chevy II mentioned earlier so I could pay the bill.

When the day of the operation arrived, I was prepped by a young tech, who proceeded to shave me not only in the area of my incision but all around my genitalia using a straight razor. He was black, and considering the tense relationships I had experienced in Vietnam and the number of angry young black men I had lived beside, I suspect my blood pressure might have become a good deal elevated, though I didn't move a muscle. Please understand that this reaction on my part was solely a reflection of my then-limited interactions with African Americans, very few of whom had shown much interest in being convivial with me. I wouldn't have the same reaction today.

MaryAnne, naturally enough, was very anxious about my surgery. She just wanted it to be over and wanted me back in good health. While the operation was taking place, she waited up in her room at the guesthouse. She understood that she probably would not be allowed to see me until the following day. That was very difficult for her to accept, but the military is not famous for flexibility when it comes to their rules, so what can you do?

Once I'd recovered from the anesthetic, the surgeon explained what he had encountered. "In your kidney we found some cysts, which we unroofed," he said. (The idea of kidneys having roofs was a new one to me.) "And since your kidney had become a small gravel factory, we also cleaned all that out. That's all that was required. I'm pleased to tell you that you still have two full kidneys." Needless to say, I was delighted about that, as well as by having the mystery of my kidney issues finally cleared up.

I considered this to be really good news despite the fact that their valiant efforts—very much appreciated, I hasten to add—had left a scar that wound all the way from the left side of my back to the left front of my abdomen. The next day, when they wanted me to get out of bed to try to walk, I was afraid I'd fall in half. But I was young and healthy and healed very quickly. MaryAnne was by my bedside each day. The operation was behind us, Vietnam was soon to be a memory, and life was good.

MaryAnne and Matt on the beach, **1969**

21

WELCOME THE NEW ARRIVAL

MaryAnne's friend Paula, once a coworker back in Napa, lived in Hawaii—her husband, John, was in the navy and stationed there. Going home to the mainland for the holidays, they were kind enough to let us use their small duplex in Kailua, about 20 minutes from Honolulu, while they were away. The timing couldn't have been better. Now, we wouldn't have to spend Christmas in the hospital. They even left us their car and a decorated Christmas tree. To this day our gratitude for their kind generosity has not diminished.

In the times when I was feeling well enough, we made good use of the car to search for housing. We quickly learned that my private's pay didn't go far in Honolulu, but we finally found a small one-bedroom apartment on Akepo Lane, in a poorer part of town. Well, it wasn't really a lane; it was actually an alley, complete with potholes, trash and shabby buildings. But it was what we could afford, and we were happy to have it. The apartment was on the third floor, which concerned me considering MaryAnne's condition.

I overheard the Hawaiian apartment manager speaking

to the Asian apartment owner on the phone when we asked for the apartment. She said, "They are *haoles* (white people), but they look okay." I have to admit, I found that moment jarring. I'd never before been on the receiving end of any kind of racist comments. Unable to imagine what it would feel like to experience such remarks day in and day out, I began to have more empathy for the guardedness of TP and other African Americans.

The apartment was unfurnished and all our belongings were on the mainland. We contacted our parents and asked that they put together a large care package of sorts, containing housewares, kitchenware, a crib and other essentials. We realized that it would take some time to fill such a crate and send it over by boat. The fact that my stepdad worked for a packing company definitely helped. Earlier, we had asked our folks to send the Toyota by ship. It arrived a couple weeks after we rented the apartment.

In the meantime, I started work as planned. We were able to borrow a couple of very basic army cots, silverware, an old dresser, an ironing board, and kitchen utensils from the army. Dr. Halperin loaned us a small couch. At mealtime we sat on the couch and lowered the ironing board far enough to use it as a dining table.

On a trip to the PX—the post exchange, where military members and their families can buy goods at discount prices—we bought a portable radio so that MaryAnne didn't have to sit in silence each day while I was at work. We weren't yet able to afford a TV. We did have some books, and I think MaryAnne read practically everything that Kurt Vonnegut had written up to that point. We also stocked up on everything the baby would need: soap, towels, and cloth diapers, the only choice at the time. I should add that despite our calling him (or her!) Matthew, we didn't know the sex of the baby until delivery—again, there was no choice about that.

I had not been receiving paychecks since I left Vietnam. While we waited for them to straighten out my pay records, MaryAnne and I were living on loans from the army. A letter from Tom, still in Vietnam, explained the mix-up. It seemed that my outfit in Vietnam believed I was a deserter since I had never returned from R&R. As far as they were concerned, I had been AWOL for a couple of months. Apparently someone along the paper trail had dropped the ball, and my transfer had never been completed.

This snafu with my records would ultimately mean that my promotion to corporal would be delayed by several months. It would also prevent any promotion to sergeant unless I stayed in the army longer than required, which I definitely didn't plan to do. Needless to say, given that promotion came with a raise and we needed every dime, I was far from happy when I learned of the mix-up. I couldn't believe that the army would make me pay such a price for its error. But, of course, that's just what happened. We shrugged and made the best of it. There was nothing to be done.

There are some things, however, that cannot be stopped by paperwork errors, and the birth of a baby is one of them.

Eventually the baby was 10 days overdue. Each day was filled with anticipation, excitement and concern as I departed for work with sweet hugs and fond farewells. While I was at work, I thought about Maryanne sitting alone in the apartment with no one to visit with while she waited for the child to arrive. Finally, on February 5, 1970, I had just arrived at work in the Psychology Service when I got a call from MaryAnne saying that her water had broken and it was time.

I went dashing home. Once MaryAnne was in the emergency room, a doctor took a quick look at her and ordered someone to take her to maternity immediately. We were both anxious and excited, though of course my anxiety and excitement didn't come with labor pains. MaryAnne recalls that a long string of chairs lined both sides of the hallway in the maternity ward. Many of the chairs on both sides were filled with pregnant women waiting to see a doctor. Maryanne was shown to a hospital room with two beds and a curtain in between.

At that time, hospitals didn't allow fathers in the delivery room. I was only allowed to see her a couple of times that day. Rather than sit in the waiting room, I spent the remaining time in my office, about three minutes away in another part of the hospital, trying to work despite my distraction.

Despite Maryanne's efforts and drugs intended to start contractions, none commenced that day. In the evening the doctor determined that a Cesarean delivery would be necessary. Around 10 p.m. I was informed that the preparations had begun. I understood little more than the basic outline of a Cesarean procedure. The idea that my wife and child would undergo this surgery was terrifying. I could only rely on the fact that uncounted numbers of women had been through this, it was standard medical procedure, and we both wanted what was best for the baby. I only got to see MaryAnne briefly before the operation, and we assured each other that all would be well.

It was far too late to be at work, but I had to do something to keep myself busy. I had one of those model car kits, which in this case contained the pieces of a Model A Ford. I spent an hour or two putting the model together. Finally, I got a call that the baby had been delivered. Matthew Graham was a healthy 7 pounds, 8 ounces, and both he and MaryAnne were fine.

Thrilled and relieved, I hurried over to the maternity ward to see him and MaryAnne. We were both grateful that, being the spouse of a member of the staff, she was moved to a room of her own and we were granted some privacy.

She was extremely tired, groggy, in physical discomfort and emotionally drained. But of course she was very relieved at the wonderful outcome. I, on the other hand, felt like a slacker, given that my entire part in the birth was just some stress, worry, and work on a model car.

According to the practices of the time, mothers with Cesarean deliveries were not allowed to see their babies until the following day. MaryAnne had been warned of this prior to surgery. Even understanding that she was exhausted and vulnerable, it seemed a silly rule to me. I was able to see Matthew through the window at the maternity ward. He was clearly a beautiful child. Of course, he looked pretty much like thousands of other infants, but to me he looked spectacular. A son—my son! He had all the requisite fingers and toes and was very alert. I was impressed with him already.

The nurses kept my visit with MaryAnne brief, but we were both on top of the world with our son's arrival. We couldn't stop grinning.

Since I was the only relative within 2,500 miles of Tripler,

MaryAnne had no company besides the occasional nurse and me. When I showed up early the next morning, she and I walked down to look at Matthew through the nursery window. She was clearly frustrated that she couldn't hold the baby at that moment, but later that afternoon they brought Matthew in to spend the afternoon with her. She was elated and bursting with joy and I was pretty much beyond words. I stayed with her as much as they would allow. By the following day, Matthew was staying in the room with MaryAnne around the clock and she was completely responsible for his care. She naturally missed having her mother and other relatives there, but Matthew seemed to keep her quite occupied and they were obviously bonded.

The first time I held him, the feeling was indescribable. He was so new, so vulnerable and so innocent. I had never been so excited, but I was also struck by the enormity of the responsibility I was facing as a father. I knew nothing about being the father of a newborn—fathers were seen as pretty extraneous not only to birth but to parenting in those days, so there were none of the books or classes that orient today's dads. I had to just go with my instincts and trust that my love for my son would lead me to become the best father I could be.

After about a week MaryAnne was discharged, and I was able to bring her and our new son home at last. Our total bill from the hospital was just $12.50—the cost of her meals during her stay. Even so, our budget remained tight. Because we had no crib or bassinet, we settled on a creative approach. We pulled a drawer from an old borrowed bureau, padded it with blankets, and used that for his bed. Matthew didn't seem to mind in the least. He was a good and happy baby. Good? He was great! I hated to leave for work in the morning and couldn't wait to go home in the evening to see my boy and my bride.

Since I was the night owl in the family, I volunteered to take the late feeding. Matt and I always had special time together around midnight or 1 o'clock.

It turned out that Matthew, like many babies, didn't sleep through the night. So someone would have to get up with him until we got him settled down and back to sleep. We decided that it didn't take both of us to get up and settle him back to sleep. Alternating nights "on duty," we soon adjusted. The one who was "off" would sleep straight through Matt's cries, while the one on duty would immediately wake. As I had discovered while learning to sleep through cannon fire in Vietnam, humans are remarkably adaptable creatures.

Also like many babies, the only place Matt really liked to sleep was in a moving automobile. MaryAnne and I were often tempted to take him for a ride in the middle of the night just for the sake of the peace it would produce. Awake, he continued to be extremely alert, lively, and fun to be around.

I was astonished by how much laundry an infant could generate. Many laundromats don't permit the washing of diapers, but that wasn't the case on Akepo Lane. Mothers in the neighborhood had neither personal washing machines nor the money to hire a diaper service. We were among many who rinsed diapers at home before washing them in the laundromat machines.

Living on the third floor made MaryAnne's frequent trips to the laundromat difficult, as she was unable to carry both the baby and the laundry up and down three flights of stairs at once. Sewing a strap onto the laundry bag let her carry it over one shoulder and the baby on the other hip, but it still wasn't easy for someone less than five feet tall who weighed five pounds less than nothing.

The large care package we had been waiting for finally arrived. Our families had filled a 3' x 3' x 4' packing crate and we were delighted with every item, from a small portable crib to a sewing machine to a lot of smaller but no less useful items.

By now we were well acquainted with just how much work it is to care for an infant 24 hours a day, seven days a week. With no friends or relatives close by to give her a break, MaryAnne had a new understanding of exhaustion.

But mostly, being a dad was wonderful. Each day was full of new and exciting lessons in caring for Matthew. For instance, when changing a diaper, leave a portion of the wet diaper draped across the boy's groin while you get the dry diaper ready. This will avoid having him spray you unexpectedly. It only took me one mishap to learn this lesson. There was also the matter of learning to put a cloth over my shoulder before trying to burp him. So many simple things that you just don't know if you haven't dealt with an infant. Every day, something new. It was fabulous when he learned to smile and then to laugh. We loved every minute of it.

Life on Akepo Lane was going pretty well until I came home from work one evening to find an elderly woman lying in our alley. A mugger had thrown her down while he was taking her purse, and she had a wound on her head where it had hit the asphalt. I took her to the closest emergency room for treatment. For me, the incident underlined that Akepo Lane was in a pretty rough part of town. The knowledge caused me very real anxiety when I thought of MaryAnne having to walk down that alley headed for the laundromat, carrying our baby while simultaneously burdened by load of clothes. She never had what one might consider a negative encounter, but that didn't stop me from worrying.

Happily, the hospital had an office of Social Services that helped married GIs find housing. They understood our situation and kept an eye out for a better place for us. After a few months we were able to move to the newly built Moanalua Hillside Apartments. In addition to being much safer than Akepo Lane, the complex was closer to Tripler. I could breathe a lot more easily, no longer fearing for my family's safety while I was at work.

We didn't have much money, but the beach was free and it became our major recreation. So there we were, this brand new family, living in an island paradise with lush green vegetation, lovely sand, the warm beautiful ocean and eternal sunshine. Still, we longed for home. We knew it would not be long before we would be returning to the support of friends and family and the familiarity of California.

It was strange to realize that I wouldn't be returning to Vietnam and my outfit. I felt my share of guilt as I thought of my buddies, for whom the war continued. But I didn't miss the heat, the mud, or the fire missions. I didn't miss the dark void, the knowledge in the back of my mind that something very bad could happen at any time. I didn't miss taking part in a war I could never believe in.

Two phone calls helped me get a bit of closure. My buddy from basic training and artillery training, Ron Principe, called me during a brief stopover as he headed home. He was fine and had talked with our friend Jarrold Brown, who was doing fine as well. And Tom Villano called on his way home, too.

It was great to hear their voices and know they too were coming home whole.

22

AIN'T GONNA STUDY WAR NO MORE

While MaryAnne dealt with diapers, bottles and a new baby at home, things were going well for me in the Psychology Service. My office was well appointed and spacious, with large windows looking out on the tropical landscape. With a steady workload of testing to perform on a wide variety of military personnel, I was becoming proficient in administering intelligence tests as well as other personality tests. Though the tests I administered were standardized, the men we tested were each as unique as all human beings are. Some were compliant and cooperative. Others would prove to be guarded and difficult. It was challenging to persuade such men to put their best effort into the task at hand. Even at its most challenging, my new work—done in comfort and with no enemy in sight except human maladjustment—was unimaginably, and wonderfully, different from my last "job" in Vietnam.

My relationship with Dr. Halperin was both educational and enjoyable. He was an excellent mentor, generous with his time and expertise, taking time each week to instruct us in types of mental assessment and in the process, honing our knowledge and careers. I appreciated working under someone so knowledgeable. I still marvel that I would probably not have had the chance to work under him had I not gone to Vietnam and from there to Hawaii and a military hospital.

After I had worked for him for a few months, I had the opportunity to repay him for his mentorship and take on a new challenge. For many years, Dr. Halperin had wanted to take his wife to Scotland, where they both had ancestral roots. But he hadn't felt comfortable taking more than a week off at a time. The day when he took me to the colonel in charge of Psychiatry and Psychology and told him I could run the Psychology Service for three weeks while he was in Scotland was a red-letter day for me. I had repeatedly been given leadership opportunities while in the army, but this was a real surprise and a serious demonstration of his faith in my competence and trustworthiness. His plan approved, off they went to the Highlands. They had a great trip, and on my end all went well with the office. I was careful to focus on that part of the testing workload with which I was most familiar. My fellow psych tech, Bob Fibigger, had left the service a couple months before, so I was helped by a new one, Boysen Palmer. Boysen was a delightful Southern fellow with a fair complexion, horn-rimmed glasses and a mellow disposition. He was truly a fine person and I enjoyed working with him.

A notable memory from my time at Tripler is the week Dr. Halperin sent me to the Presidio hospital in San Francisco to learn about tests that assess brain damage. MaryAnne and I were able to come up with enough money to purchase tickets, so she and Matt could come along with me. It was the only time that year that we were able to get a visit with family in Napa. Of course, MaryAnne and I were pretty much overlooked, however benignly, in the midst of the fuss made over Matthew. He was the first grandchild for both my parents and MaryAnne's. As for him, after living a quiet life with just his mom and dad, he was suddenly surrounded by nine members of MaryAnne's family and five members of mine. He seemed to love the attention. It was a wonderful reunion, but it only made us miss our families and home more.

The months went by, and, as the end of my tour of duty approached, I found myself with mixed feelings. For years, I had focused on how much I didn't want to be in the military. But to my surprise, as my time got short I found myself with some trepidation. Strange as it sounds, I was leaving complete job security, not to mention the monthly paycheck that supported us. And I was stepping back into a world I'd only just begun to understand when the army had pulled me away from it. Would I succeed or fail there? I didn't yet know, and the lack of certainty sometimes felt scary.

For the first time, I foresaw the mental readjustment that would take place as I left the world of the military. In war, one tries to stay sane in an insane situation. My fellow soldiers and I had been placed halfway around the world, in an environment where the rules we had lived by all our lives had been changed and where the bottom line rule was, "Do what you need to do in order to stay alive and keep your buddies that way." That's why we would speak of "going back to the world," back where the rules of daily living seemed to make more sense. You leave the insanity behind as best you can. Just as the rules had changed when I entered the military, they changed again when I was released, leaving me to adjust once again.

As my release date approached, it was natural to reflect on the past few years. The time spent in the military had been an adventure, even though not one I had asked for or one I would seek out again. But despite its frustrations, neither was it one I would trade for any other. In those two years I had learned a lot both about the world and about myself. I had met and dealt with people from many different backgrounds, most of whom were very decent human beings, many of whom had added to my personal growth, and some of whom had given me both friendship and enjoyment. My time in the military had tested and matured me, challenging me in ways that bolstered my self-confidence as well as my self-awareness. In the end, I saw my military service as pretty much a tossup. Whatever it was that I might have missed seemed more than adequately balanced by all that I had gained. I had few regrets about the army. I was just ready to move on to whatever lay ahead.

With the learning gained from a great mentor and some work in the field under my belt, my ambition to become a psychologist was stronger than ever, and I was increasingly able to see that ambition as a realistic one. I looked forward to using my G.I. Bill benefits to help pay for a master's program that would improve my prospects and knowledge even more.

Most importantly, my romance had blossomed into a marriage and my marriage had blossomed into a family. I was learning to be both a husband and a father while experiencing all the joys of both roles. It was a relief to know that I enjoyed and could handle the responsibility. MaryAnne and Matthew were the center of my life, and I could no longer imagine living without them.

Because I'd made it clear I planned to return to college immediately, the army agreed that I was eligible to leave the service a few months early. Any GI worth his salt, and certainly any draftee, knows the ending date of his contract with Uncle Sam. Some months before my exit date I received army paperwork offering me the opportunity to re-enlist. I gave it due consideration for about a second and a half—all the time I felt it deserved—and responded, "No." I was officially moving on.

All that was left to work out were the logistics. I was accepted for the master's program in psychology at the California State University at Chico. Realizing that I would leave Honolulu and reach Napa only one day before I had to begin classes if I entered in the fall semester, I opted to wait a few more months and begin in the spring. The delay would be good for my little family, giving us time to find housing in Chico, move our belongings, and get settled before the semester began. I went to the hospital's personnel office well ahead of time to make sure the paperwork would be done appropriately. As eager as we were to get back to the mainland and our families, I can't say it was any great sacrifice to stay a couple months longer in Hawaii! There are definitely worse places to wait.

It was curiously fitting that the day I got out of the army was also my mother's birthday. It was she who had at first encouraged me to serve my country; she who then later told me I could leave the war; and she who wrote me some of the most meaningful letters I received, keeping me updated on family doings and encouraging me spiritually.

When the date for my exit from military service finally arrived, MaryAnne and I were excited and anxious to see friends and family again. Still, it was difficult saying goodbye to friends at Tripler. Boysen and I had worked well together and it was tough leaving him without an immediate replacement, but he would get help soon. I had taught him my job and he was up for the challenge. The more difficult farewell was with Sidney Halperin, who had taken me under his wing and nurtured my interest in psychological measurement. It was clear that he was finding my leaving difficult, even though he wanted only the best for me. I was sad to bid him goodbye.

The army helped us pack up our belongings and we returned borrowed furniture and housewares. I was booked on a military flight from Honolulu to Travis Air Force Base in Fairfield, California, while MaryAnne and Matthew took a commercial jet to San Francisco. Family picked us up in both locations and brought us together for the happy homecoming. There was a joyous gathering at MaryAnne's parents' house, and to top it off, it was Halloween, and as I've said, my mother's birthday. No tricks were played but there were plenty of treats. The biggest treat, of course, was all being together again.

Later that evening MaryAnne and I took Matthew home to the mini-ranch. As I drove down the long dusty drive to our cottage, I was struck by the memory of the many times we had approached that humble home. This time was different. The war was behind us, our child was asleep in

MaryAnne's arms, and a bright future lay ahead.

It was only a couple of months before I would enter graduate school, so our arrangements were all temporary. The snafu over my army salary had finally been resolved and my back earnings paid. By law I was getting my old job back, working the night shift stocking shelves in the grocery store. MaryAnne would be staying home with Matthew, who was changing and growing by leaps and bounds.

Once again I would be driving north on Highway 99, moving our belongings to a new home and looking forward to a graduate program. After two years we had come full circle. Yet despite the familiarity of so much of what I was doing, the core of my life had changed. The threat of Vietnam and the draft no longer hung over me, casting fear and uncertainty on every aspect of my existence. Unlike so many of my fellow soldiers, I had the ultimate privilege: that of coming home whole. With my wife and son in my thoughts, I was determined to savor every moment of that good fortune.

EPILOGUE

RETURNS AND REFLECTIONS

During World War II, troops coming home from Europe took a boat for an ocean crossing, which provided them with some days to decompress with their buddies and get used to the idea of being back in the U.S.A. Vietnam vets got on a plane and were walking down the street in a U.S. city in one day. There was little in the way of time for adjustment before they found themselves home and once again in civil society. When they reached home, many found an angry and ungrateful group of citizens waiting at the airport, intent on pointing out to the troops the shame they should be feeling. Some demonstrators called returning vets "baby killers," cursed them and spit on them.

Though it feels hard if not impossible to understand now, this denigration of those who sacrificed to fight should probably be seen in light of the fear, grief and frustration so many felt about the war; the brutal and often militaristic response to anti-war protest, at Kent State and beyond; and the government's lack of response to a nation pleading for peace. But I'm immensely glad that this period of blaming the troops who fought an unpopular war is unique in our history. Sadly, we continue to fight wars, but at least we now show more respect for those who risk their lives fighting our battles.

Though dwarfed by the carnage of the World Wars, the two-decade conflict in Vietnam had a heavy human toll. The U.S. estimates that 200,000 to 250,000 South Vietnamese soldiers died in the conflict. In 1995, when Vietnam finally released its own official estimates, it put total North Vietnamese and Viet Cong fighter deaths at 1.1 million and civilian deaths at 2 million.[2] As many as 300,000 Cambodians and 62,000 Laotians also died in the course of the conflict.[3]

As the divisions of opinion caused by the war healed, the U.S. military's sacrifice was better recognized and honored by the American people. In 1982, at the Vietnam Veterans Memorial in Washington, DC, 57,929 Americans were listed as dead or missing as a result of the war. Their names are inscribed on the wall in chronological order, with space left for late additions. Since 1982, the number of names on the wall has grown to over 58,000, largely as a result of later deaths due to injuries sustained in Vietnam. Of the 3,403,400 U.S. military deployed to Southeast Asia,[4] 75,000 were deemed severely disabled and more than 23,000 100% disabled; 61% of those Americans who died in the war were under 21 years old.[5]

This story has focused on the men in the war, including myself. But I can't close without mentioning the approximately 11,000 women who served in Vietnam. Of these, roughly 90% were nurses. In 1984 the Vietnam Women's Memorial was completed to honor them.

As this book suggests, military deaths and physical injuries don't fully convey the cost of the conflict. Some estimates put the numbers of American draft evaders admitted to Canada during the Vietnam conflict as high as 30,000 to 40,000.[6] Families were bitterly divided, even permanently estranged, in disagreement over the war. Many soldiers who looked uninjured later suffered a variety of debilitating and even fatal symptoms, possibly caused by chemicals such as the defoliant Agent Orange. Others, who also seemed healthy enough when arriving home, suffered from the invisible wounds of what is now called Post Traumatic Stress Disorder (PTSD), a psychological disorder for which there was as yet little understanding and no effective treatment. Self-medicating with drugs and alcohol and unable to hold jobs, many ended up homeless or committed suicide. In his best-selling book *What It is Like to Go to War*, Karl Marlantes points out that while the military trains you on how to fight and kill, they don't train you on how to live, later, with the reality of the violence you may have experienced in combat.[7] It's not surprising that so many veterans struggle when returning from war, even today.

The toll taken on American service people and their families of what might be called "collateral damage" from Vietnam can never be accurately or precisely assessed. Neither can the war's impact on the country's unity or confidence in its leaders' integrity.

As I said earlier, I was exceptionally fortunate. I came home to a welcome unmarred by bitter hostility and with my body, my spirit, my marriage, my prospects and my self-confidence intact. To this day, I try never to forget just how privileged that made me.

I was also lucky to have a parent who encouraged spiritual search and reflection from early on. My mother taught me that although a person can harm another person's physical body, the "victim's" soul cannot be killed. I may slow a person's progress by killing his body, but my act will not destroy the essence of his being or prevent his ultimate advancement. Each of us finds our own way to deal with fearful responsibility. Maybe the beliefs just mentioned are simply my mechanism for making war bearable. I have no doubt that the guns I manned killed people, and my beliefs don't prevent me from carrying my share of guilt and regret for the undeniable harm of which I was a part.

My story is uniquely mine, and I am lucky to be able to tell it. There are hundreds of thousands whose Vietnam stories will never be told. Some were not able to tell those stories, while others have chosen not to do so. The stories of yet others died with them in the midst of war. It may well be that, as David suggested, I agreed to take part in that war due to a debt I had to pay or lessons I had to learn. In view of all that I experienced and all that I learned, I would have no difficulty either arguing David's case or arguing the side of those who hate me for my participation.

One thing I am certain of, however, is that this true story contains a number of twists and turns that take it in surprising directions. For some, such surprises may be put down to nothing more than coincidence. My own perspective on them is different. When I see a coincidence or two, I say, "What are the chances of that happening right at that time?" But when I see a much longer series of coincidences that all lead to an outcome that has been predicted, I stop dead in my tracks and wonder, "How is this possible?" That's where I am today, left looking back on this period in my life.

Consider the story told here.

A car accident totaled my vehicle, yet did nothing more to me than have me end up facing in the opposite direction from my academic goal.

On the very same day I arrived home to find my draft notification.

Once I was in the army and ordered to Vietnam, Elsie predicted that I would not finish my tour in Vietnam but rather would be sent to an island.

I was picked "at random" to accompany TP on his exit from the army, which gave us the opportunity, however briefly, to find some kind of peace with one another.

I received David's declaration that the bonds that kept me in Vietnam no longer had power over me. After several weeks, I made a decision that I was done with the war and made a brief prayer saying that I was ready to leave. Three days later, the unexpected chance of the R&R arose, to a coveted destination that for some reason no one else in the entire unit seemed to want but me.

A kidney stone attack on my second day of R&R brought me to Tripler Hospital in Honolulu, and the diagnostic anomaly I presented delayed my return to Vietnam.

A job offer suddenly appeared, one that included a transfer out of the artillery and into the very profession I had dreamed of, at a location where my wife could choose to join me and we could be together for the birth of our first child—all as was predicted in the cards.

For the record, I admit to believing in some universal

energy, some immensely powerful force, that is far greater than humans. Whatever that power is, I do not picture it as an old man with a beard sitting on a throne. Given the choice between a universe based on chaos and chance versus one based on some form of order, I come down on the side of order, given the laws of physics and my own perceptions of the universe.

As for a personal *raison d'être,* the only purpose I can find to justify my existence is to learn, grow and evolve to some higher state. Without claiming that I have made any lofty progress in that direction (progress that I tend to think takes many lifetimes), my experience before being drafted and then in the war itself could be said to serve that kind of growth well. Limited options, difficult choices, battles within and without: all are things that surely try, but may well also refine, the evolving soul.

Today, I still can't say whether I did the right or wrong thing in going to war rather than choosing one of the other equally difficult options. I only know that I fought the internal battle and came to my decision as courageously as I could, and that my inner struggle as well as my experience in and beyond the "real world" war changed me in ways for which I am grateful.

APPENDIX

ABOUT THE 110 HEAVY HOWITZER

The 110 heavy howitzer is the largest cannon that was used in Vietnam. It fires a 204-pound projectile that is about 3 feet long and 8 inches in diameter. Thus it is often referred to as an "8 inch." The gun is a separate-loading cannon, which means the projectile and the explosive that propels it are each loaded into the gun separately.

Each projectile (requiring two men to carry it) was carried on a metal rack the short distance (roughly 20 feet) to the back of the gun, where the carrying rack would hook onto a hydraulic ram. The ram would then place the shell in position and drive the shell into the proper location in the tube. Packets of separate loading powder would then be placed behind the projectile and the breach closed. A blank cartridge roughly the size of a .45 caliber bullet was then placed in the breach, at which point a lanyard was attached to the firing mechanism. A warning, which gave men the chance to cover their ears, would be called out just before firing. The army provided earplugs, but it seemed that few people used them. They were painful and not very effective. Men often used cigarette filters, which seemed to work better. The tube would be swabbed with water after each shot was fired to insure that an ember from the previous shot would not set off the next powder packet prematurely.

We were not the only guns at Charlie 2. Other sections of the base had 175- and 155- millimeter batteries. These are somewhat smaller cannons. The 155 cannon fires a shell approximately 6 inches in diameter, the 175 cannon a shell approximately 7 inches across. We never really had much contact with the guys on those guns, so my understanding of them is limited.

The 110 heavy howitzer fires a variety of shells, including one that goes off on impact, one built for piercing concrete, one with a timer that allows it to go off before the shell actually strikes the ground or any other surface, and a firecracker round that fires numerous smaller explosives. We fired mostly those that went off on impact and occasionally those with timers.

We got a special treat if the target of a fire mission required the use of a "charge five." As noted earlier, the explosives used in an 8-inch howitzer are loaded separately behind the projectile. The explosive is packaged in seven packets. If a certain two of those packets are removed and five are left, the remaining "charge five" propels the projo such that it breaks the sound barrier just as it leaves the muzzle of the cannon, thus greatly increasing the noise and the intensity of the muzzle blast. (This is opposed to a charge 6 or 7, in which the sound barrier breakage occurs within the tube, a much less dynamic event.)

Of course, this brief overview necessarily simplifies a complex and technical subject. I encourage those who are interested in these guns to seek out some of the many excellent detailed discussions available today on the Internet.

AUTHOR'S NOTE AND ACKNOWLEGEMENTS

In selected instances I have chosen to change the names used for purposes of privacy.

I wish to acknowledge Jarrold Brown, Ron Principe and Pete Langenbach for their support and friendship during training. Thanks to Tom Villano for helping me laugh through grim times in Vietnam. Thanks to Cork Kennedy for hours of proofreading, valuable editorial suggestions, and 50 years of friendship.

Deep gratitude to Matt Graham for creating the book cover art as well as the signpost image. Thanks as well to Suzanne Karp for her first-rate work on the half-century-old photos in the book and to CJ Madigan of Shoebox Stories for designing the book.

Special recognition goes to my mentor Suzanne Fox of BookStrategy for her help, knowledge, guidance, humor and priceless support.

Deep and heartfelt thanks go to my wife MaryAnne for her ongoing feedback, support and patience.

And one final note: TP, if you are out there, you take care.

ABOUT THE AUTHOR

Don Graham left the army in 1970, returning to California with his wife MaryAnne and his infant son Matthew. A second son, Timothy, was born in 1972. In 1973, Don completed a master's degree in counseling psychology; he received a doctorate in educational psychology in 1978.

Don worked for several years running the Office of Testing and Research at the California State University at Chico. In 1982, he accepted the position of Director of Psychological Counseling, Wellness and Testing at the university.

From 1985 to 1990, MaryAnne and Don worked diligently in Beyond War, a peace-oriented movement founded in 1984.

In 2004, Don became the university's Associate Vice President for Student Affairs, a position he held until he retired from the University in 2007.

Today, he and MaryAnne live in Sonoma County, California, in the "Valley of the Moon." They greatly enjoy activities with both of their sons, Matt and Tim, and their sons' families, all of whom live in Santa Rosa.

END NOTES

1. David Bruton, *The Unknown God Revealed,* DeVorss & Company, 1951.
2. Please note that statistics from the Vietnam War can be calculated using different assumptions and also change as new information becomes available, additional deaths deemed to have resulted from the war occur, etc. For that reason, all figures given here are provided only as indicators of the scope of the war; they are subject to change and should be re-checked in more current sources rather than being relied upon. Figures from Britannica.com, https://www.britannica.com/event/Vietnam-War.
3. Wikipedia, https://en.wikipedia.org/wiki/Vietnam_War#cite_note-Obermeyer_2008-52, various sources.
4. https://www.va.gov/opa/publications/factsheets/fs_americas_wars.pdf.
5. https://www.uswings.com/about-us-wings/vietnam-war-facts/.
6. Valerie Knowles, *Forging Our Legacy: Canadian Citizenship and Immigration, 1900–1977*, Chapter 6, "Draft-Age Americans in Canada" section (no pages listed). Public Works and Government Services Canada, 2000.
7. Karl Marlantes, *What it is Like to Go to War*, Grove Press, New York, 2011.

www.ingramcontent.com/pod-product-compliance
Lightning Source LLC
LaVergne TN
LVHW051116080426
835510LV00018B/2062